BERMUDA
AND THE AMERICAN
REVOLUTION: 1760-1783

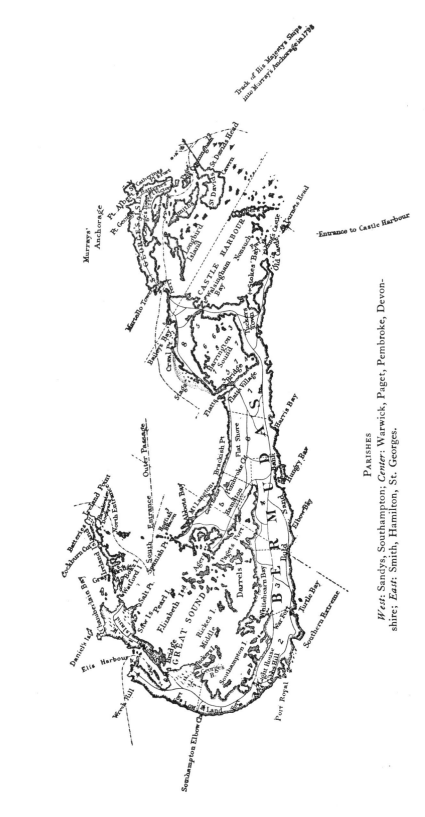

Track of His Majesty's Ships into Murray's Anchorage in 1795

Murrays' Anchorage

Entrance to Castle Harbour

Ft. Albert
St. Catherine
Ft. George St. George's Town
Smith's Id.
St. David's Head
St. David's
Gurnet's Head
Martello Tower
Longbird Island
Ferry
CASTLE HARBOUR
King's Castle
Walsingham Bay
Nonsuch
Stokes Bay
Gates' Id.
Old Castle
Bailey's Bay
Crawl Pt.
Tucker's Town
Sluice
Harrington Sound
Flatts
Bridge
Black Village
Harris Bay
Brackish Pt.
Flat Shore
Pembroke Ch.
Hungry Bay
Gibbs Bay
Mt. Langton
Hamilton
Harbour
Sand
Elbow Bay
Turtle Bay
Ireland Point
Cockburn Cut
North End
Outer Passage
Spanish Pt.
Gibb's Id.
Batt. cr.
Goose Bay
Welford
Darrell's
Southern Extreme
Chamberlain Bay
Girland Id.
Salt Pd.
Agar's
Paget's Port
Whitechurch Bay
War Fort
South Entrance
Daniel's Id.
Saw Id. Pearl I.
Elizabeth Id.
GREAT SOUND
Rickes I.
Port Royal
Ellis Harbour
Bridge
Middle
Tucker's
George's
Southampton I.
Light House
Gibbs Hill
Wreck Hill
Long Land
Southampton Elbow Church
BERMUDAS

PARISHES

West: Sandys, Southampton; *Center*: Warwick, Paget, Pembroke, Devonshire; *East*: Smith, Hamilton, St. Georges.

BERMUDA
AND THE AMERICAN
REVOLUTION: 1760-1783

BY
WILFRED BRENTON KERR

ARCHON BOOKS
1969

SBN: 208 00794 6
LIBRARY OF CONGRESS CATALOG CARD NUMBER: 69-19216
PRINTED IN THE UNITED STATES OF AMERICA

PREFACE

THE AMERICAN revolution was a movement by no means confined to thirteen colonies. The measures of reorganization undertaken by the British government in the period 1760-1765 affected all the colonies of British North America; and protests against the Stamp Act arose from Quebec to St. Kitts. After the repeal of that act, most of the colonies—by a numerical computation—abandoned opposition and resumed the status quo. Thirteen went their own way and eventually separated from the empire. The non-revolutionary colonies were deeply involved in the conflict of 1775-1783. Some of them had minorities anxious to throw in their lot with the revolting Americans; some were fields of military operations; some viewed the war chiefly as it affected their commercial interests. These colonies have not altogether escaped historians; the invasion of Quebec in 1775-1776 is a familiar theme and of late years the fortunes of Nova Scotia have received some attention. But of the others scant notice has been taken. It is the hope of the present writer to be able to investigate conditions in the non-revolutionary colonies and suggest reasons for the attitude in each case toward the national movement in the thirteen. This book, which may be the first of a series, contains the results of such a study with regard to Bermuda, which by reason of its carrying trade was linked most closely of all to the colonies in revolt.

The author is glad to acknowledge his debt to the Bishop of London for permission to use the papers in Fulham Palace; to Dr. Henry Wilkinson for aid in research and valuable advice on Bermudian affairs: and to Mrs. G. P. Coleman for facilitating in every way the consultation of the letters in Tucker House.

CONTENTS

SOURCES

THIS study is based almost entirely on manuscript sources, Bermuda having been rather a
neglected island in historiography. The writer has
used the following collections.

1. The papers in the Public Record Office, London,
concerning Bermuda of the revolutionary period. The
correspondence of the governors with the Board of
Trade and the Secretaries of State for the Colonies
are contained in the C. O. 37 series, chiefly vols. 19,
20 and 36-38. Certain instructions and commissions
are found in C. O. 38 vol. 10. The minutes of legislative council and assembly are for the most part in
C. O. 40 vols. 15 and 18 but occur also in extracts in
the 37 series.

2. The correspondence of the Bishop of London
with the Anglican clergy of Bermuda, contained in
the Bermuda packet, Fulham Palace Library.

3. The correspondence of St. George Tucker pre-
served in Tucker House, Williamsburg, Virginia,
and made accessible to the public by the courtesy of
Mrs. George P. Coleman. Here are several hundreds
of letters and other documents from the Tucker
family in Bermuda to St. George in Virginia which are
most valuable for the purpose of this book.

4. The archives of Bermuda, which have been
searched for me by Dr. Henry Wilkinson, historian of
the founding of the colony. For the period under review these contain of importance only the minutes
of executive council, of which considerable use has
been made.

5. The papers of the Continental Congress in the
Congressional Library at Washington. These con-

tain a number of petitions from Bermuda which are of use.

The Admiralty Office papers yielded nothing, the letters from Captain Jordan of the *Nautilus* having apparently disappeared. The correspondence of General Gage in the S. L. Clements library in Ann Arbor, Michigan, may contain two letters from the governor of Bermuda; but as the librarian has informed me, it is not yet available to the public.

The principal printed sources of value are the Journals of the Continental Congress and the Letters of Members of that body which contain much information about the relations of the United States and Bermuda. W. F. Williams's *History of Bermuda* has some traditions of interest; and A. E. Verrill's *Relations between Bermuda and the American Colonies* has yielded some details. Other books and manuscript sources are cited in the footnotes. The contemporary newspapers on the continent have been searched almost in vain.

CHAPTER I

THE ISLAND AND THE ISLANDERS

Hail! Nature's darling spot, enchanted isle
Where vernal blooms in sweet succession smile
Where cherished by the fostering sea-born gale
Appears the tall palmetto of the vale.
The rich banana, tenant of the shade
With leaf broad-spreading to the breeze displayed,
The fragrant lime, the lemon at its side
And golden orange, fair Hesperia's pride
The memorable tree of aspect bold
Which graced thy plains, O Lebanus! of old. . . . [1]

BY the time of the American revolution, the Bermuda islands had been settled for one hundred and fifty years. They contained a white population almost purely English in origin, and in 1760 largely native as immigration from home had long been negligible. In 1774 there lived on the islands 5632 whites, 5023 blacks; in all, 10,655 persons.[2] These had at their disposal a soil generally rocky and sandy but in many regions, especially of the main island, of a good red earth. The fertile areas were capable of sustaining the inhabitants if Governor Bruere's view was correct; they "will produce almost anything we may sow or plant with little trouble."[3] In fact they did yield to some of the islanders potatoes, barley, coffee, lemons, oranges, onions and a little

[1] Nathaniel Tucker, *The Bermudian*, in F. C. Hicks, *Bermuda in Poetry*, p. 31. Hamilton, Bermuda; Colonist Press, 1915.
[2] Governor George James Bruere to Earl of Dartmouth, March 29, 1774. C. O. 37 vol. 36.
[3] Bruere to Board of Trade, September 17, 1765, in C. O. 37 vol. 19, and November 6, 1773, in C. O. 37 vol. 36.

wheat and cotton. Of the land held by private owner-
ship, however, only one-tenth was thus cultivated.
Half of the rest furnished pasture for cattle and a few
horses; the other half was covered with cedars. The
cleared land was occupied by the inhabitants in farms
of fifty acres each in average, forming narrow un-
fenced strips on which they tied their horses and
cattle.[4] But agriculture made only a limited appeal to
the Bermudians and was practised chiefly in the center or country parishes, Devonshire, Pembroke, Paget
and Warwick, the first of which is without a harbor.
These contained one-third of the population, farmers
and others. In all, provisions were raised in sufficient
quantity to support the islanders for only three
months in the year. Some Bermudians, especially "of
the meaner sort," found or supplemented a livelihood in the excellent fisheries close at hand. But even
this obvious occupation was not in high favor.[5]

For the Bermudians, sons of a sea-faring race, had
found the conditions of the islands singularly adapted
to stimulate the traditional spirit of adventure. Being, moreover, "people of excellent natural parts"
they had early sought business of a more remunerative
and less humdrum nature than agriculture and fishing.[6] Internal commerce was indeed hardly worth
mentioning; in 1764 Bruere found "no market but
their method is to kill a sheep and borrow and lend a
joint when opportunity or conveniency offers."[7] Of

[4] "The lordly bullock there, unused to toil
   Securely stalks the tyrant of the soil."   (*The Bermudian*, p. 35.)
[5] Bruere to Board of Trade, September 17, 1765, in C. O. 37 vol. 19; to
Earl of Dartmouth, November 6, 1773, in C. O. 37 vol. 36; Papers of John
Bridewood in C. O. 37 vol. 38.
[6] The Rev. Alex. Richardson to Bishop of London, June 23, 1766, in Fulham Palace Papers, Bermuda packet.
[7] Bruere to Board of Trade, 1764 undated, C. O. 37 vol. 19.

much more importance was the craft of shipbuilding. Bermudians had early discovered their native cedar to be at once so light and durable as to make the best sailing ships in North American waters. They built sloops and brigs (sixty in 1764, thirty-five in 1774) and sold them in the West Indies or North America.[8] Ship carpentry therefore gave employment to a fair number of men, especially of the east end around St. Georges, and it was supplemented by the business of ship repair, as Bermudians were willing to accept wages on behalf of themselves or their slaves which reduced costs to one-third of the customary rate in the West Indies. With the art of shipbuilding went that of navigation, which far surpassed any other in the favor of the islanders; and eighty to a hundred vessels were constantly at sea, each manned by a skeleton crew of two whites and four negroes. Some of the boats were owned by their captains, a good many by better-off islanders who employed the crews. In this way fully half of the able-bodied men became expert mariners. These were for the most part dwellers in either end of the island group but especially in the east from which access to the open sea is easy and direct.[9]

The carrying trade therefore had become the peculiar business of Bermuda. Some of the inhabitants took the little spare produce of their country, ducks,

[8] "The sturdy craftsman with laborious hand
    Fells the tall tree and drags it to the strand
    Resounding shores return the hammer's blows
    Beneath the stroke the gaudy pinnace grows
    Launched and completely manned in quest of gain
    Spreads her light sails and tempts the watery main."
                                  (*The Bermudian*, p. 35)

[9] Bruere to Earl of Dartmouth, November 6, 1773, cited above; the Rev. T. Lyttleton to same, undated 1775 in C. O. 37 vol. 36.

Halifax

Boston

New York

Philadelphia

Bermuda

Charleston
Savannah

St Augustine

Bahama Is.

Cuba

Hayti

San
Domingo.

cabbages and onions, to St. Eustatia, Santa Cruz, Curaçao and other foreign ports of the Caribbean, or failing these, to the British colonies such as Barbados and Antigua. As alternative to the produce they might take Bermuda soft limestone, in some demand through the West Indies as material for building in spite of its porousness. Having disposed of their cargoes, they might seek for passengers and freight up and down the West Indies and finally return home with rum, tea and calico. The poverty of island products, however, strictly limited this export and barter business. Most of the seafaring Bermudians were compelled to seek elsewhere for their stock in trade. They resorted to the Tortugas and especially to the Turks Islands, and there they raked salt in the first months of the year for sale to passing American vessels or use as cargo.[10] Thence they would proceed to South Carolina or Virginia in quest of corn or to Philadelphia or New York in order to exchange the salt or money for such necessaries as flour, salt pork, beef, peas, lumber and candles. From the continent some of the islanders would proceed directly home; others would sail to the sugar colonies, dispose of their American provisions there for cash, reserve a sum for a new cargo to the mainland and put the rest into bills of exchange to be used for purchases in England. In these ways the Bermudian mariners made a living and some of them grew rich. They dealt with Americans not only on the continent but in Bermuda itself; for New England vessels brought most of the wheat used in the islands, taking in payment the dollar pieces of eight and Portugal money from the West Indies. Thus the

[10] Bermudians had occupied the Turks Islands in the last quarter of the seventeenth century, had lost them to the Spaniards and had recaptured them in 1710 under the leadership of Lewis Middleton.

Bermudians procured the provisions which they could not or would not grow for themselves.[11] Certain islanders indeed found occupations of a more occasional and less laudable nature; they took advantage of ships wrecked on the reefs to the north and west in order to "salve" their cargoes by methods closely resembling those of Dick Turpin. A few even sailed to dangerous places like the reefs of the Cacos; and trusting to their own great skill in navigation and to their light sloops, lay in wait for the wrecks of less fortunate vessels than their own. Such practices led Governor Bruere to inveigh against his islanders as "wild and savage-like,"[12] and they were only too well condoned by many inhabitants.

Hence in ways legitimate or not, "every person in these islands whether in power or not, are concerned in trade more or less."[13] Other persons were also concerned in trade; His Majesty's customs collector and staff of searchers whose task it was to examine the cargoes of incoming ships and levy duty according to

[11] The Rev. T. Lyttleton to Dartmouth, above; Colonel Henry Tucker to Undersecretary B. Thompson, February 22, 1781, in C. O. 37 vol. 38; Bruere to Earl of Hillsborough, August 18, 1770, in C. O. 37 vol. 34.

> "But early torn reluctant from their home
> Amidst the tempest's roar condemned to roam
> Thy scattered sons, a race of giant form
> Whose souls at peril mock and brave the storm
> At honest labor's call with fruitless pains
> Are far dispersed o'er Britain's wide domains."
> (*The Bermudian*, p. 32)

Henry Tucker, Sr., thus described the condition of the maritime trade: "Though perhaps the owners of vessels themselves may be no great gainers by this trade, it supports all our seamen whose wages alone amount to near £30,000 per annum," exclusive of returns from the salt. To St. George, July 31, 1774, in Tucker House Papers (cited hereafter as T. H. P.).

[12] Bruere to Hillsborough, December 28, 1768, in C. O. 37 vol. 33 and April 27, 1772, in C. O. 33 vol. 35.

[13] Bruere to Board of Trade, November 30, 1764, in C. O. 37 vol. 31.

the laws of trade and navigation on commodities from foreign parts. But Bermudians bent on bringing in rum, tea and calico from those foreign parts had no fondness for this habit of the King's officers. They had early realized the natural advantages of their islands in that "every creek of the island and indeed it abounds with them, was a port of entry where they did what they pleased"; and they set their habitations in such manner as to use these informal ports of entry without benefit of customs. Even merchants and mechanics disposed themselves in "promiscuous settlement" leaving the town and principal harbor of St. Georges "almost deserted."[14] Thereby they obtained great strategical advantage over the customs officers and worsted them in many battles of wits.

Nevertheless the customs collector and his staff were not ciphers. From time to time they did catch sloops engaged in smuggling, and by confiscating the cargoes persuaded some Bermudians that payment of duties was the less of two evils. Further, although islanders bringing in goods for immediate consumption might evade the officers and take no more thought about the matter, the owners of sloops employed in the export or re-export business knew that customs clearances had a very definite value in ports of destination like New York or Philadelphia, and could be procured only from the officers. Bermudians were therefore in two minds about the customs officers, not being able to live with them or without them. In these circumstances the location of the official port of entry was not a matter of indifference, since the comings and goings of the vessels increased business at that port. The people of St. Georges desired a monop-

[14] Lieutenant Beard to Board of Trade, January 28, 1765, in same volume.

oly of customs for their town, those of the center and
west clamored for permission to enter at Crow
Lane[14a] and Ely's Harbor as well. The question of the
ports of entry remained the chief topic of internal controversy and the principal cause of embitterment
between the capital and the rest of the island.

Almost half of the dispersed population consisted,
as we have seen, of negroes. In spite of a scare of
revolt in 1762, the blacks were usually docile and a
considerable number became baptised. One slave out
of eight worked on the farms; the others, trained by
their masters, were ship carpenters, coopers, black-
smiths and seamen. Bermudians reckoned their
wealth by the number of their slaves and had increased that number to a point dangerous for a country which relied on importation for three-fourths of
its food supply. The negroes when hungry stole vege-
tables from the gardens and thus injured even the
little cultivation which was practised. But slave own-
ing produced its worst result in the depreciation of
the status of manual labor and the morality of the
masters; and however industrious the Bermudians
were abroad, at home they became notably indolent.
"The great number of slaves," declared Bruere in
1779, "which are now kept by the poor white inferior
people of these islands have sapped the foundations
of respect and obedience to government in the white
people by their authority over the slaves which gives
a certain imperious behaviour in the master or mis-
tresses very unbecoming in any exalted station and
much more so in any necessitous white persons who
ought to work themselves for their support and not
depend on a negro to pick up a nail or a pin or carry

[14a] Crow Lane is the present Paget and Crow Lane Harbor is Hamilton
Harbor. Note of Dr. Wilkinson.

away a small quantity of provisions."[15] When the lifting of household articles proved unworthy of a white man, cultivation of the soil became positively degrading.[16] Hence racial prestige raised the traditional habit of distaste for farming to the intensity of an obsession. The "kind of Paradise" which Bruere had found in 1764 remained to a large extent "without art, cultivation or agriculture"[17]; and aversion to the soil, devotion to overseas trade and addiction to the feud with the customs officers remained the underlying motives in Bermudian political life of the 1760's and 1770's.

The determination to maintain and if possible increase wealth in the form of slaves and the other determination not to raise food for them at home made livelihood precarious for many Bermudians. The spectacle of distress was no unfamiliar one in the islands. In 1765 a limited emigration took place to East Florida; and the Rev. John Maltby wrote approvingly of the plan "as we have so many hundreds living badly nay rather perishing very miserably. . . . This island seems to be running fast to destruction and the people, it is probable, will be very greatly distressed." His colleague, the Rev. Alex. Richardson, a year later expressed himself in much the same strain "My parishioners are miserably poor."[18] These worthy

[15] Papers of John Bridewood, cited above; Bruere to Earl of Hillsborough, August 18, 1770, in C. O. 37 vol. 34; Bruere to assembly, May 12, 1779, in C. O. 40 vol. 20 (assembly minutes); Silas Dean to Continental Congress April 26 to May 1, 1776, in P. Force, American Archives, Fourth Series, V, 1083-5.

[16] A. E. Verrill, *Relations between Bermuda and the American Colonies during the Revolutionary War*, p. 47. New Haven; publications of Yale University, 1907.

[17] Bruere to Board of Trade, undated 1764, C. O. 37 vol. 19.

[18] The Rev. John Maltby to a merchant of South Carolina, January 23,

clergymen were writing in the depth of a post-war slump as well as making special pleas; and they may not have intended to portray such conditions as normal. But at all times the livelihood of many Bermudians depended seriously on events external to the islands, on fluctuations of commerce or political developments which might expose trade to hostile action. No islander could be indifferent to the relations of Great Britain with other great powers.

Bermudians were well aware that they were members of a great empire. The British navy and a garrison had safeguarded them from French and Spanish depredations as late as the Seven Years War; and though an independent company of troops had been disbanded in 1763 a detachment of the 9th Regiment remained until 1772 as a visible symbol of imperial protection. The islanders had commercial dealings with the mother country; they bought thence most of their imports of manufactured goods such as sail duck, nails, cordage, linens and woollens to the extent of £15,000 a year.[19] But they exported almost

1765, in C. O. 5 vol. 540; the Rev. Alex. Richardson to Bishop of London, June 23, 1766, cited above.

The emigration was organized by Messrs. Ephraim and John Gilbert. One hundred families expressed an interest in the project but only if they could settle at harbors suitable for trade. The fertility of the land in East Florida provided no attraction. The Gilberts therefore rejected the tract set aside for them by Governor Grant and chose Amelia Island and the banks of the Nassau and St. Mary's instead. About seventy families left Bermuda; they encountered a sickness at Sunbury, Ga., and the survivors reached the St. Mary's at the end of 1767. (Governor James Grant to Board of Trade, March 1, 1765, and enclosure, July 16, 1765, January 26, 1766, in C. O. 5 vol. 540; August 5, 1766, November 27, 1766, and to Earl of Shelburne, October 31, 1767 in C. O. 5 vol. 541. A few from the St. Mary's joined the Americans in 1776 (Governor Patrick Tonyn to Germain, July 1, 1776, C. O. 5 vol. 557). Whether these were Bermudians is not certain but appears likely.

[19] Bruere to Earl of Dartmouth, November 6, 1773, in C. O. 37 vol. 36.

nothing in return, making payments in bills of exchange obtained in the West Indies. Hence they had little in the way of direct business relations with their fellow subjects of the British Isles. Nor did their few merchants resort to Great Britain or send their children home for education to anything like the extent practised by the British West Indians. Intercourse with the mother country was at all times slight.

In one respect the Bermudians followed the model of the homeland; the great majority belonged to the Church of England. There was indeed a Presbyterian congregation in Warwick and a small one at St. Georges; but this last "hath for some years been so visibly on the decline that there was great room to entertain the agreeable hope that in a few more years all the inhabitants of these islands would have been of the established church."[20] The Rev. Alex. Richardson, the "little bishop" of St. Georges, in eleven years baptised a thousand children, white and black, increased the number of his communicants "to a wonderful degree" and brought it about that his church was beautifully sashed and a steeple built.[21] The Church of England has always been a loyal institution par excellence and in praying for the King, the Queen and the royal family, the parishioners doubtless felt a bond of sympathy with their fellows of the motherland. But the habit of seafaring much reduced the attendance and the interest of the men and in consequence the influence for loyalty of the Church of England. "A regard for religion is not a characteristic of the Bermudians," declared a resident. "They

[20] The Rev. T. Lyttleton to the Crown, June 1775, Fulham Papers, Bermuda packet.
[21] The Rev. Alex. Richardson to Bishop of London, June 23, 1766, cited above.

seldom go to church except it be to attend a funeral
or to get their children baptised or to hear a stran-
ger."[22]

Certainly it had never entered the heads of Bermudians to consider themselves other than English-
men or their membership in the empire other than
advantageous. The ties of race and the need for protection inclined them by first impulse to follow Great
Britain's lead. But their occupation as mariners led
at least half of the men to consort continually with
West Indians and North Americans, especially the
latter. Many sons of the best families, finding opportunities in their native land limited, went to the continent for their education and remained there to
conduct businesses or follow the learned professions.[23]
The ranks of the clergy were filled in part by North
Americans; two of the three Anglicans resident in
1755 were "bred in North America" and the two
ministers of the Warwick Presbyterian church from
1750 to 1778 (John Maltby and Oliver Deming) had
come from New York.[24] Hence the social outlook of
the islanders was in preponderant part toward the
south and west; and the Bermudas had much in common with the mainland colonies, especially of the
southern group. They had no share, however, in the
political life of the continent. The long struggle against
Indians and French, the difficulties with forests and
mountains, the Puritan jealousy of the Church of
England meant little or nothing to the islanders.
Isolated in the Atlantic, devoted to the sea together,
few enough to permit the majority to know something

[22] W. Winterbotham, *An Historical, Geographical, Commercial and Philo-
sophical View of the American United States and of the European Settlements
in America and the West Indies*, IV, 291. London, 1795.
[23] Verrill, p. 48.
[24] Richardson to Bishop of London, June 23, 1766, cited above.

of one another personally, the Bermudians had developed a stubborn attachment to their island and a family feeling for each other, though this was quite capable of interruption by bitter family quarrels. Occasional aspersions in the Tucker letters on Bermuda for its dullness, its burial of talents in indigence and obscurity and especially its lack of economic opportunity, only mask an intense concern for the interests of "our country" which means Bermuda only.[25] Thinking of themselves as British, receptive to American ways, most of the islanders were at heart Bermudians first, keenly alive to their commercial interests and unwilling in an unusual degree to sacrifice these to the requirements of sentiment. It must be added that like other men who go down to the sea in ships and occupy their business in great waters, many Bermudians failed in their statements to observe the niceties demanded by truth and honor.

The constant intercourse with the Americans and the native quarrel with the customs officers had led the islanders to hold local authority in scant esteem. "Refractory to good order" declared Bruere of them in 1772; and seven years later he confirmed his opinion. "These people notorious in running counter to government from the time of Governor Pitt." In this opposition the chief part had usually been played by "the two families of Tuckers . . . always the principal promoters and leaders of faction."[26]

The Tuckers of Bermuda were descended from a family which had possessed land in Kent and North-

[25] Henry Tucker, Jr., to St. George, December 3, 1771, April 13, 1774. T. H. P.

[26] Bruere to Hillsborough, April 27, 1772, in C. O. 33 vol. 35; to Germain, August 2, 1779, in C. O. 37 vol. 37. The two families, i.e. of Port Royal and Somerset.

ampton. St. George Tucker, born 1651, migrated to Bermuda, settled in Southampton parish and died in 1710. His son Henry (1683-1734) married Frances, daughter of John Tudor of New York. Their second son Henry (1713-1787) was the most prominent member of the family in the third quarter of the century. Known as Colonel Tucker, perhaps from a command in the militia, he was a man of fine appearance and considerable physical vigor.[27] Gifted also with shrewdness and some diplomatic ability, he was well liked and trusted by his fellow Bermudians. He had married Anne Butterfield and become father to a family of four sons and two daughters, to whom he was wont to address moral exhortations in the vein of Polonius. He lived at his country home in Southampton parish, often called Port Royal[27a]; and he engaged in mercantile ventures, the success of which he estimated once in excessively pessimistic mood: "I don't know any one undertaking for the last seven years that have succeeded with me."[28] In spite of Bruere's strictures, uttered in a time of exasperation, it does not appear that Colonel Henry and the governor were on bad terms at any time before the outbreak of the revolutionary war.

The eldest son of the family, Henry Tucker, Jr., elected to remain in Bermuda and to pursue a political career which eventually elevated him to the presidency of the council of the island. All the while his opinion of his own duties was not high. "Our assembly is now sitting," he wrote to his brother. "I am therefore necessarily engaged in public business, which I abom-

[27] A description by his grandson in J. W. Kaye, *The Life and Correspondence of Henry St. George Tucker*, pp. 4-5. London; Richard Bentley, 1854.

[27a] Port Royal, the name of a small harbor, was frequently extended to the whole parish. Note of Dr. Wilkinson.

[28] To St. George, August 14-October 18, 1774. T. H. P.

inate, and seized with Bermuda politics, which I
cannot help holding in sovereign contempt."[29] The
art of concealing sentiments, however, was that in
which Henry Tucker excelled. His wariness as a
politician is illustrated by the almost uniform lack
of color in his letters even to that brother. "An accomplished gentleman in every sense of the word" and
"of moderate views and conciliatory disposition,"[30] he
managed to retain the goodwill of all and at the same
time to discharge effectively the various duties which
fell to his lot throughout the difficult period with
which we have to deal. Next to him were Thomas
Tudor Tucker and Nathaniel, both of whom finally
elected to study medicine and attained the degree of
M.D. The first settled in Charleston and after the
usual troubles of a beginner, including a quarrel which
almost brought on a duel, was practising his art with
some success in the early 'seventies. His brother
Nathaniel joined him there in 1772 but did not remain. In fact he preferred literature to physic and
read Gray and Goldsmith to the family circle. From
admiration he proceeded to imitation and in 1774
brought out a poem, *The Bermudian*, from which we
have quoted freely. He went to Edinburgh in the same
year, studied medicine there and finally settled as a
physician in Hull. His youngest brother St. George,
born 1752, went from the Rev. Alex. Richardson's
school to the College of William and Mary in Williamsburg in 1771. Having graduated the next year, he
remained in Virginia until 1775, studying and practising law and incurring expenses which drew a running fire of parental reprimands. Colonel Henry's
family thus illustrates by its dispersion the attraction

[29] To St. George, March 10, 1775. T. H. P.
[30] Kaye, 1-2.

of Bermudians to the continent in the eighteenth century.

This family was of course not the only one of the name in Bermuda at the time. Other descendants of the original St. George Tucker had made their homes in various parts of the islands; and among them at this time was another Henry Tucker, born 1736, son of a former Chief Justice John Tucker who had built Bridge House[31] in Sandys parish.

This man was known accordingly as Henry Tucker of Somerset. He was not strong physically, being ill during practically the whole period 1772-1774; but mentally he was active beyond other members of the Tucker group. He read much, especially in the political literature of the time, and became a liberal in theory, ascribing the insurrection of Caribs in St. Vincent in 1772-1773 much too hastily and confidently to the greed for land of the whites. An opportunity was soon given him to pass from the theory of politics to the practice. When able to resume his seat in the assembly after his illness, he made it his first business to procure certain payments from the public treasury to his relative Nathaniel, in high indifference to the prior claims of more needy creditors.[31a] Thus it appeared that if government in St. Vincent should serve the supposedly weaker party, in Bermuda it should serve the undoubtedly influential. Liberalism was in fact merely a veneer over Henry's real interest, the acquisition of a fortune for himself. Versed in

[31] Bridge House is a substantial Georgian structure about sixty by fifty feet with two storeys; it is now the rectory. (Information supplied by Dr. Henry Wilkinson.) Henry Tucker of Somerset was elected to the assembly in 1769.

[31a] The favor to Nathaniel in a letter to St. George, October 30, 1774, T. H. P. Nathaniel had been clerk to the council 1768-1772; his appointment is in minutes of executive council, June 7, 1768.

subtle ways and in the art of managing men, he made himself master of the petty Tuckers at the Bridge, John, Dan, Robert, James, and master of policy in the west end. He possessed an entire lack of scruple and a sense of humor, both of which served him well in his enterprises. He came into close connection with the family at Port Royal by his marriage to Frances, daughter of Colonel Henry; and he soon acquired much influence over his father-in-law. By their comparative wealth, their connections and their personal abilities, the Tuckers enjoyed a considerable influence on the island. Through their members on the continent and the associates of their business there, they made themselves well acquainted with the currents of opinion in the colonies concerning relations with Great Britain.

The government of Bermuda was similar in structure to those of other groups of British islands. The Board of Trade sent out a governor who usually remained for a long period; Bruere had the helm of state for sixteen years. The council consisted of ten members appointed as vacancies occurred by the home authorities, ordinarily on nomination by the governor. That official, however, had only a limited field of choice; men of birth and education being none too many in Bermuda, he was compelled to select from a narrow circle, ordinarily the well-to-do residents of St. Georges. The assembly was composed of thirty-six members elected from the nine parishes. But the number of men available to serve was greatly reduced by the practice of seafaring and by the expense of staying in town during session; country members accepted their duty reluctantly, came late and went home early. The Bermuda assembly thus constituted had habits peculiar to itself, chief of which was a high indifference toward the function of attendance. Only rarely could the quorum of fifteen be obtained on the nominal day of meeting, for which reason Bruere thought the number should be reduced to twelve; adjournments were necessary for months at a time and when a legal house did meet, its muster was likely to be less than twenty. Occasionally the governor dissolved the assembly for non-attendance; but as usually the same men were reelected, he effected no cure of their political malady. Governor Popple tried this expedient in 1763 but could not induce the new house to meet and at the end of three months was compelled to dissolve them again.[32] The condition was aggravated by differences among the members; each group could always paralyze the others by the simple process of absenting itself. And finally, individual members were not slow to realize their importance in such circumstances; "[they] either attend or not as any rules or orders relative to trade may please or displease them."[33] Hence the legislature of Bermuda functioned but in lame and halting fashion at the best.

Attendance, however, was easiest and least expensive for the men of the capital. The direction of the assembly therefore at such times as it chose to function tended to remain in the hands of the group elected from St. Georges and its vicinity. As this group came from the same circle which furnished the councillors, it exercised powerful influence in both bodies of the legislature. A few merchants and shipowners normally controlled the affairs of Bermuda; "the House is at present under the direction of two or

[32] Bruere to Board of Trade, September 1, 1766. C. O. 37 vol. 31.
[33] Bruere to Board of Trade, July 18, 1765. C. O. 37 vol. 19.

three merchants" as one officer wrote.[34] This leading group was closely related by intermarriage; in 1768 Thomas Jones of the council had a son and two sons-in-law on that body beside him. The leaders had their own ways of managing the governor, impressing their views on him in social intercourse and exercising pressure if necessary by letting his salary fall into arrears and making them up if his conduct were satisfactory. They of course used the power thus acquired for the benefit of themselves and their friends, annexing whatever places of honor and profit lay in the gift of the local government and taking first options on economic opportunities arising from the conduct of public business. Most notorious of these was the affair of the crown lands near St. Georges which had long been occupied by forty poor families. In Popple's time the home authorities decided to sell these lands and gave instructions to that effect providing for a preference to the squatters. But the three commissioners appointed by governor and council to take charge of the sale ignored this aspect of the instructions and disposed of the lands to themselves and their friends. One of the three, George Forbes the councillor, sold himself Paget's Fort Island without even a reservation of the fort.[35] Favoritism of this nature rather than peculation was the practice of the men of St. Georges. Other Bermudians naturally viewed such proceedings with disfavor, suspected peculation as well, resented the governor's adherence "more particularly to the ever-prevailing party of St. Georges" and conceived a hatred for that town

[34] Lieut. Beard to Board of Trade, January 28, 1765, cited above.
[35] The Rev. T. Lyttleton to Dartmouth, undated 1775, in C. O. 37 vol. 36; George Bruere to Lord George Germain, December 12, 1780, in C. O. 37 vol. 38.

which on one occasion inspired the expression of a doubt whether they would defend it if it were attacked.[36] The animosity in such extreme form was transitory but it illustrated the jealousy which west and center entertained toward the east as a harbor of plotters for monopoly. Though with sufficient determination they could have clipped the wings of St. Georges, they found it more difficult to make the effort than merely to maintain the dislike. Hence in spite of carpings and mutterings, the well-to-do of the capital retained their domination.

The standing problem of Bermudian government was that of finance. A tax of 16 d. currency on each £100 of real estate had been allotted to payment of the governor's salary. But warm-hearted assessors took pains to prevent this burden from weighing too heavily on their friends and neighbors; and the governor rarely received his full due.[37] The tax would not have produced a great deal of money in any event as the majority of Bermudians were far from affluent;[38] but no doubt if properly levied, it would have produced more than was actually the case. The legislature allowed a light duty on horses and slaves to expire; and the whalers, who were supposed to pay fees on their catches to the governor, ceased to do so of their own volition in 1768. The crown lands yielded £353 a year, at the time of the revolution, of which £150 was appropriated to the salary of Attorney-General Dan Hunt, the rest to that of the deputy secretary and provost marshal, John Randle. A duty of 2¼ d. per gallon on rum had once

[36] Bruere to Board of Trade, December 6, 1764, in C. O. 37 vol. 19.
[37] Bruere to Dartmouth, June 18, 1774, in C. O. 37 vol. 36.
[38] The Rev. Alex. Richardson to Bishop of London, June 23, 1766, cited above.

been the mainstay of the revenue.[39] The home authorities, however, had prohibited the import of foreign
rum in the interest of the British West Indies; but
crafty Bermudians imported it as usual by their own
methods. Thereafter not one gallon in ten came in
legally to pay the duty; and the public income from
this source shrank in proportion. The total of duties
received at the customs house of St. Georges in 1769,
including those on liquor, did not reach £300. A great
gap developed between revenue and expenditure,
modest as the last was (£433 a year, exclusive of the
governor's salary). The chief justice, Jonathan Burch
and the judge of the court of vice-admiralty, John
Esten, perforce contented themselves with fees; but
the inferior officers of government in the court of
assize and the quarter courts, the clergymen, the merchants who furnished supplies to the public, struggled
with each other for drops from the trickle of Bermudian revenue.[40] Governor Bruere replied to a complaint by the Rev. Thos. Lyttleton that he had received no salary. "The other two ministers have not
and in short none of the officers of government have
from the door-keeper of the house of assembly and
their clerk up to the governor who has now above
£600 due to him."[41] Salaries were years in arrears;

[39] The assembly had laid an additional 3 d. a gallon on rum in 1762 to pay
their salaries but repealed it in 1770. This duty dated from 1698 with varying
amounts.
[40] Bruere to Hillsborough, May 10, 1769, C. O. 37 vol. 20; to Dartmouth,
November 6, 1773, C. O. 37 vol. 36, and June 9, 1774, same volume.
[41] Bruere to Lyttleton, October 9, 1771. Fulham Palace Papers, Bermuda
packet.
   The Rev. Alex. Richardson had received £30 a year and a plate at his
table from Governor Popple, but gave it up, "he being a man of libertine
principles and having a disagreeable housekeeper." Bruere did not continue
the bounty, having "a large family and his attention fixed on it." To Bishop
of London, June 23, 1766. Fulham Palace Papers.

two clergymen quit the islands in despair of receiving remuneration; merchants who sold materials to the government found it a labor of Sisyphus to try to obtain payment. Elementary public conveniences like roads, bridges, the landing at the main ferry stood in permanent need of repair. The "civil watch" was neglected throughout the islands; many jurors from the country did not attend when legally drawn because they could not bear the expense of being in town and received no reimbursement.[42] Bermudian public finance was conducted less on British or American principles than on those of poverty-stricken countries. It was therefore no easy task which awaited the governor of Bermuda at the time of the American revolution.

[42] Presentment of the grand jury in minutes of executive council, December 1, 1773. Bermuda archives.

CHAPTER II

GOVERNOR BRUERE
AND THE ASSEMBLY 1764-1774

GEORGE JAMES BRUERE arrived in Bermuda as governor in succession to William Popple in September 1764. An old soldier and a veteran of Culloden, he had obtained his post in part as a reward for his services in the field. To a grandson he appeared remarkable for his demonstrations inspired by potations; but it does not appear that he looked upon the wine when it was red to a greater extent than was customary for a gentleman of that time.[1] He has left in Bermuda a reputation for irascibility; the documents reveal unfailing loyalty, ability of the average order, kindliness to the poor,[2] some shrewdness but a too frequent uncertainty and lack of ingenuity in dealing with opposition.[3] His family which eventually reached fourteen in number occupied perhaps an undue share of his attention and certainly kept him in

[1] "I remember to have seen him after rather copious libations, go through the evolutions of the battle of Culloden and other great fights in which he was personally engaged. He marched and counter-marched—charged the enemy with great vigor—handled his large stick with great skill and effect—and generally concluded with the shout of victory—the 'British Grenadiers' or the popular anthem of 'God Save the King.'" Kaye, pp. 7-8.

[2] Occasionally he gave permission to certain poor inhabitants to violate the fishery laws in order to obtain badly needed food "out of pure humanity and charity to the poor people," as he claimed. Bruere to Earl of Hillsborough, April 4, 1772, in C. O. 37 vol. 35, enclosing the assembly's complaints and his answers.

[3] In response to one appeal from Bruere for stricter orders to the Bermudians to abstain from plundering wrecks, the Earl of Dartmouth stated that he could not guess what Bruere meant by assuming that orders from London would halt the islanders. Had he not punished them? Dartmouth to Bruere, August 3, 1774, in C. O. 37 vol. 36.

financial difficulty. Among the governors of Bermuda it would be easy to find some better, some worse. Shortly after his arrival he summoned the assembly. That body, filled with hope at any change, appeared in better humor than usual and voted him £400 currency (£265 sterling) as his salary. Second thoughts presently suggested regrets that they had not first extracted some concession relative to illicit trade. Thomas Jones, councillor and treasurer, wrote to New York to seek advice on the status of the assembly, hoping by a declaration of its illegality to circumvent the appropriation. Failing, he sought to make a little capital by representing the confirmation of the assembly's status as a strengthening of the governor's position. But Bruere saw through the plan and concluded that he could place only limited trust in his councillors. He next encountered difficulty from certain J. P.'s of the center, including Thomas Dickinson, who wanted to hold quarter sessions at a small public house near Crow Lane and for that purpose to bring the prisoners ten miles from St. Georges. When Bruere and Attorney-General John Slater objected to this excessive regard for their own convenience, they all resigned. He was compelled to fill their places with councillors whose theories of duty were fully as liberal as those of Thomas Jones.[4] Such were Bruere's first lessons in the art of politics as practised in Bermuda.

In accord with instructions from home about additional duties shortly to be laid, he imagined it his chief task to reduce the amount of illicit trade indulged in by his islanders. That the inhabitants refused to assist the customs officers even if summoned by magistrates was perhaps a phenomenon of

[4] Bruere to John Pownal, January 11 and July 11, 1765. C. O. 37 vol. 31.

little novelty to an eighteenth century Englishman.[5] More serious was the discovery that sloops were permitted "to go in to divers creeks, corners and little harbors . . . under the pretence that vessels might load and unload at the west end provided it was under the inspection of a searcher who upon enquiry I found had been dead many years." Bruere promptly issued a proclamation directing all vessels to come to St. Georges for inspection, after which they might proceed up-country or to sea. Six vessels sailed at once from the west end in open defiance of the order; and the assembly united in a remonstrance, the country members professedly desiring a second port of entry, those of St. Georges entertaining fears for a cargo of clandestine goods on a Dutch ship in Town Harbor under the collector's nose. Ignoring the last aspect of the problem, Bruere gave some consideration to the first and decided in favor of a measure already under discussion for opening Crow Lane in addition to the capital. The assembly accordingly passed a bill to this effect; but the councillors, residents by majority of St. Georges, blocked it.[6] Thus pending decision by the Board of Trade, the capital was established as the only legal port of entry into Bermuda; and the inhabitants, who had considered the matter of ports settled by Popple's indulgence, were "astonished and

[5] Before Bruere's arrival, the collector had induced the officer commanding the troops to send a party with a lieutenant to the west end to aid him in his enforcement of the duties. The west enders promptly refused quarters to the troops, who were obliged to return. Bruere to Board of Trade, November 30, 1764, in C. O. 37 vol. 31.

[6] Bruere to Board of Trade, November 30, 1764, and to Pownal, January 11, 1765, in C. O. 37 vol. 31; petition of the inhabitants of St. Georges, December 6, 1764, in C. O. 37 vol. 19. The searcher mentioned was Thomas Butterfield who died in 1761. Popple's excuse for not appointing another was that the office of searcher was "rather a screen for illicit trade than a preventive of it." To Board of Trade, August 12, 1761, in C. O. 37 vol. 19.

exasperated."[7] Bruere soon realized that he had ir-
ritated the sore spot of the body politic; not so soon
that he had renewed the quarrel between St. Georges
and the rest of the island and had stirred up a controversy which kept him occupied for eight years.
Eventually he appointed a searcher, John Stiles, for
the west end and thereby further displeased the
people of that locality.[8]

While the question of ports and the fresh orders
against established commercial practises were the
talk of the island, the Stamp Act took effect. The
Bermudians had refrained from the disorder which
had preceded that act in New England and even as
far afield as St. Kitts. In the first days of November
1765, those islanders who had business requiring
stamps voluntarily called for them, their first impulse
being to obey the imperial authority. Word spread,
however, that vessels with stamped papers would
meet a hostile reception in continental ports; and the
body of merchants came to see Bruere "desiring that
their vessels might be allowed to clear out without
taking the stamp papers, saying that their vessels
might be burnt or destroyed by having the stamp
papers on board, by refractory people in some of the
other colonies." Bruere in response could not admit
that the possible violence of law breakers was any
excuse for infringement of the law. "I gave them a
decisive answer that it was out of my power to dis-
pense with, mitigate or alter any resolutions of the
British Parliament; and that they would find their
advantage by keeping trade open and their vessels

    [7] W. F. Williams, *An Historical and Statistical Account of the Bermudas*,
p. 80. London 1848.
    [8] Bruere to Earl of Shelburne, April 28, 1767, in C. O. 37 vol. 31: minutes
of executive council, March 19, 1765. (Bermuda Archives.)

employed till we should hear from England." The merchants acquiesced, returned to the country and made use of the stamped papers to clear their sloops. Bruere nevertheless was no advocate of the act in itself; on the eighteenth he advised the council to address His Majesty "with hearts full of duty and affection" and to plead that the stamps were "too great a burden" for the small trade of Bermuda.[8a]

But as it became clear that twelve of the colonies were successfully defying the imposition, the sympathy of Bermudians for the continentals took its effect. They refused the stamped papers for law business and thereby perhaps facilitated one act of violence. "Some few stamp papers from the secretary's office with law business were taken from the messenger and destroyed in the country; which put a stop to that business, the jury refusing them." The last clause is obscure but apparently means that in the absence of the papers the jury would not go on with the case, thereby showing itself of different temper from that of juries in New England. No one repeated the defiance; but the magistrates made the prevailing uneasiness a reason or excuse for neglecting to enforce the license laws concerning retail of liquor. The members of the assembly had recourse to their favorite weapon; in May of 1766 rumor had it that they would not meet until the Stamp Act was repealed. Even the news of the repeal, arriving shortly afterward and broadcast by Bruere through the clergymen in the churches, mollified them only partly; as late as October, they had given "very little attendance" upon public business, "being disgusted at the

[8a] That the petition was sent appears from a news item in *Boston Evening Post*, February 10, 1766; but it is missing from the C. O. records.

Stamp Act" and waiting for determinate orders concerning their center of trade. The act had been carried out only in respect of clearance papers. No constitutional issue was raised, Bermudian concurrence in exercises of imperial authority being unquestioned in theory, imperfect only in practise.[9]

Before the stamps had been forgotten, the Townshend Act came into force (November 1, 1767). Two years later the assembly boasted "we have ever been careful to avoid the unhappy disputes that have subsisted between the Parliament of Great Britain and the colonies" and expressed pious wishes for the restoration of harmony. The claim was justified, the method of avoidance having been that congenial to expert smugglers. The duties "on glass, red lead, white lead, painters' colours, tea and all sorts of paper . . . do not amount to more than £23 for these two years past . . . in this government and give the traders an infinite deal of trouble" wrote Bruere in 1769. The payment of £23 in two years could hardly rank as a major economic grievance; and their sense of identification with the empire prevented Bermudians from regarding it as a sentimental one. Toward the end of 1769 Bruere received word of a change in the policy of the home government; and he at once informed the council that His Majesty's ministers entertained no design to lay further taxes upon America for the purpose of raising a revenue but intended soon to take off the Townshend duties as contrary to the true principles of commerce. The disappearance of the duties, except that on tea, in 1770 made little difference to Bermuda; and the retention

[9] Bruere to Board of Trade, May 1, 1766, in C. O. 37 vol. 19; to Hillsborough, July 24, 1768, in C. O. 37 vol. 32. Minutes of executive council, November 18, 1765, and May 6, 1766. (Bermuda Archives.)

of the tax on tea caused no controversy and no theoretical opposition, islanders being entirely occupied with the practical.[10]

All this time, governor, council and assembly had engaged in a series of disputes arising out of the difficulty about ports and the ensuing friction among sections. The country members, departing for once from their customary acquiescence, made serious efforts to shake off the control of the well-to-do group in the capital. They thought to go over the council's head by appointing an agent in London who should move the Board of Trade, and passed a bill to that effect; but the council defended its position by a prompt rejection. They next sought the governor's cooperation; and with his consent and that of the parishes, passed a measure to allow vessels to load and unload at Crow Lane after inspection at St. Georges. But the council still stood in the way. The assembly in bad humor now made difficulties about finding barrack equipment for the troops; and, trying a new tack, assumed the power to pass accounts without reference to the other branches of the legislature.[11] Bruere thereupon dissolved them (October 1768) and in issuing new writs sought to improve attendance by limiting the choice of candidates to persons present on the islands. St. Georges led off with a protest against this invasion of the liberty of the electorate; and the newly chosen representatives of the other parishes joined in asserting the illegality of their status. Others have on occasion loudly demanded the

[10] Assembly minutes of November 3, 1769, in C. O. 40 vol. 15; Bruere to Hillsborough, May 10, 1769, in C. O. 37 vol. 33; minutes of executive council, October 4, 1769. (Bermuda Archives.)

[11] Bruere to Board of Trade, March 23, 1767, in C. O. 37 vol. 20; to Shelburne, May 18, 1767, in C. O. 37 vol. 31 and November 15, 1767, same volume; to Hillsborough, October 20, 1768, in C. O. 37 vol. 20.

right to be represented; Bermudians were now de-
manding the right to choose absentees, or not to be
represented. When to the disapproval of the islanders
was added that of Lord Hillsborough, Bruere abandoned his plan and left the assembly free to follow its
peculiar traditions.[12]
    Bruere was by no means the tool of the clique of
St. Georges; he had endeavored to meet the assembly
halfway. But that body now fell out of humor with
him, perhaps because of his appointment of the
searcher at the west end. They allowed the arrears of
his salary to grow and ceased to provide money for
his official boat.[13] Thereby they drove him into the
arms of the council and caused him to suspect that
they partook of the American spirit of rebelliousness.
In June 1769 the assembly passed a budget with which
the council found considerable fault. On receipt of
the criticism, the representatives took fire at the supposed dictation of the dominant clique and passed a
set of resolutions denying to the upper house any
voice in money bills other than "yea" or "nay."
Bruere, now thoroughly alarmed, saw in these resolutions the temper which had inspired the Virginia
Resolves, and on advice of council dissolved the lower
house. For this action he received a mild reprimand
from Lord Hillsborough who found the resolutions

[12] Bruere to Hillsborough, December 20, 1768, in C. O. 37 vol. 20; Hillsborough to Bruere, May 13, 1769, in C. O. 37 vol. 33.
[13] Bruere to Hillsborough, May 16, 1769, in C. O. 37 vol. 20.
    In June 1769 Bruere desired to inspect the rolls of assessment on which the
tax to provide his salary was based, and enquired of council whether he had
a right so to do. The council referred the matter to Attorney-General John
Slater who pronounced that the governor might demand a sight of the rolls
but could not compel the church wardens to produce them. Being now in
position to summon spirits from the vasty deep but not assured that they
would come, Bruere proceeded no farther in the matter. Minutes of executive
council, June 21, 1769. (Bermuda Archives.)

warm and intemperate but not derogatory to the
authority of Parliament. The censure, of course,
Bruere was careful to keep to himself.[14]
The new assembly, composed of much the same
persons, met in April 1770. At that time business was
stagnant; sloops sold with difficulty if at all and in
the absence of income from this source the island was
drained of cash to buy corn for the negroes. The collection of revenues was attended with more trouble
than ever. The assembly therefore set out on the hunt
for a scapegoat among the culprits of St. Georges and
fell on the late treasurer, Thomas Jones, son of the
president of the council, who had just resigned his
office for the more remunerative occupation of going
to sea. They tried to find fault with his conduct of his
duty and to that end engaged in sharp exchanges with
the governor, who did not omit to remind them of their
own financial failings. As no evidence was forthcom-
ing that Jones had abused his position, the assembly
abandoned that line of attack and endeavored to
undermine the treasurer's position. They passed a
bill to levy an excise on rum, a tonnage duty on vessels and a tax on slaves; and for the collection of the
money they ordered the choice of two men in each
parish, for its reception they would themselves elect
a receiver-general. They thus ignored not only the
treasurer but His Majesty's instructions about the
administration of colonial finance. Bruere gave them
a lecture about the evasion of the rum duty as the
source of public penury, reserved the bill for the judg-

[14] Minutes of council and assembly and Bruere's messages, June 23-26,
1769 in C. O. 37 vol. 20 and 37 vol. 33; Bruere to Hillsborough, June 24,
1769, in C. O. 37 vol. 33 and Hillsborough to Bruere, January 18, 1770, in
C. O. 37 vol. 34.

ment of home authorities and dissolved the assembly.[15]

The technically new assembly met on November 5, 1770, and received another lecture on the nullification of the rum duty. The members, at a loss for an income but not for an argument, replied that it was the executive's business to enforce the collection of that duty. No progress was made along these lines.[16] At the opening of the next session, on March 9, 1771, Bruere argued the matter of the receiver-general with a view to showing that not in St. Kitts, Nevis, Montserrat nor indeed in the House of Commons in London had a claim been made to appoint such an official. The arrival of news that the Board of Trade had vetoed the bill now made discussion futile; no one could find anything better to utter than the complaints of two or three members that the governor's reference of the matter to London showed "arbitrary despotism." His reply was an adjournment. When they met again in May they asserted their duty to complain of grievances and to make the sovereign acquainted with "the oppression of the people." Bruere adjourned them again in the hope that they would recover their tempers.[17]

Meanwhile an event occurred which made Bruere's position easier. His eldest daughter Frances married Henry Tucker, Jr., in 1770. The marriage was happy; the new Mrs. Tucker was "an affectionate and exemplary wife" and the first child Harry was soon the apple of his grandfather's eye.[18] Colonel Henry

[15] Minutes of assembly, April 26-28, 1770, in C. O. 40 vol. 15; Bruere to Hillsborough, May 30, 1770, in C. O. 37 vol. 34 (two letters of same date).
[16] Minutes of assembly, November 9, 1770, in C. O. 40 vol. 15.
[17] Assembly minutes, March 9, 1771, May 2, 1771, in C. O. 40 vol. 15; Bruere to Hillsborough, May 4, 1771, in C. O. 33 vol. 35.
[18] Kaye, p. 8.

visited the governor and advised his son St. George that he would be welcome at Government House.[19] When St. George Tucker went to Williamsburg, Bruere wrote to him and commended his ability and his qualifications for his profession.[20] Frances Bruere Tucker enjoyed Nathaniel's discourses on literature and admired his poems.[21] The relations of the two families became most cordial and remained so until 1775. The governor now made good political use of his son-in-law; appointed him treasurer in 1770 and finding him reliable, made him councillor. In the former capacity Henry Tucker, Jr., proved all that could be desired; at his death his accounts were found perfectly clear except for a matter of £32 expended by his predecessor.[22] The influence of Colonel Henry Tucker's family was now on Bruere's side.[23]

The Tuckers were west enders; and their accession to a position of power was in fact though perhaps not in intention, a considerable concession to the opposition. But some assemblymen thought the elevation of Henry Tucker not enough; and in the session of April, Thomas Dickinson of Crow Lane and Sam Harvey persuaded the house to choose a committee of grievances of which they were principal members. They presently produced a list of complaints which laid all the ills, real or imaginary, of the island at the door of the council and governor as representative of the ever-

[19] Undated, 1770. T. H. P.
[20] December 15, 1772. T. H. P.
[21] To St. George, undated, 1775. T. H. P.
[22] Kaye, p. 8.
[23] Henry Tucker, Jr., and John Tudor took their seats in council January 15, 1771. Minutes of executive council of that date. The appointment to the treasury proposed to council, February 7, 1770, minutes of that date. (Bermuda Archives.) Henry Tucker, Sr., and Richard Jennings were securities.

dominant clique of the capital; and they published it
abroad in the hope of interesting Bermudians at large.
Bruere, who was not usually slow to argue, made
replies which cleared his own record, and sent a copy
of grievances and refutations to the Colonial Office.[24]

[24] Assembly minutes, April 3-18, 1772, in C. O. 40 vol. 18.

The complaints went back to Popple's time, when that governor had
supposedly obtained an illegal salary from an unconstitutional assembly.
The business of the crown lands naturally received much attention. The
commissioners had not only appropriated the lands to themselves and
evicted the occupiers, intended by His Majesty to have the preference, but
they had thereby destroyed the rents which had supported the matrosses
(garrison gunners) of the castle and had caused fortifications, artillery and
ammunition to fall into a state of neglect. Further, they had bought some of
the land on credit, stripped it of timber, allowed it to revert to the Crown in
default of payment, then repurchased it at low rates. Coming to Bruere's
time, Dickinson and Harvey charged that the governor and council had made
certain payments from the fund arising out of the rum and wine duty without
referring them to the assembly. The treasurer had obliged necessitous
creditors of the public to wait years for their money. The efforts of the assembly to take the management of finance out of such incompetent hands by the
receiver-general bill had been balked by governor and council. The matter
of ports was also a subject for accusation; the council had defeated all proposals to make Ely's Harbor and Crow Lane ports of entry. A number of
unrelated charges followed. The commissioners appointed to build a jail which
should also serve as a barrack had neglected their duty and put the country to
expense for quarters for the troops meanwhile. The old jail in these circumstances had gone out of repair and felons had escaped from it. The assembly
had tried to raise the standard of pilotage; the council had accepted the bill
but the governor had refused it. Further, Bruere had erred not only nega-
tively but positively. He charged fees on whales which burdened that fishery.
He had allowed some men to take small fish with a net instead of with a hook
and line as the law had directed for preservation of resources. He had discharged a man from jail without due process of law. He had removed Richard
Washington and Mrs. Riddell from their position as joint administrators of
the Riddell estate for failure to give securities and had appointed in their
stead Thomas Smith and Henry Tucker; and he was now delaying the wind-
ing up of the estate. But if Bruere were at some fault, the clique in control
were at worse. They neglected Somerset Bridge; they left vacancies in the
judgeships and the roll of commissions in the militia; they had stripped certain school lands of timber and let the teachers suffer; last, they were responsible for even the insufficient cultivation of the land.

In reply Bruere of course pointed out that he had no share in the doings of
Popple's time. The transfers of small sums from the rum and wine fund were

At the same time the assembly resumed their bill about the receiver-general and flavored it with phrases uncomplimentary to governor and council. When it came to the nomination of a receiver, however, the Tuckers struck in and John Tucker secured the choice of none other than Henry, the existing treasurer. When the assembly had thus stultified themselves, Bruere adjourned them. The leaders took their complaints to the country but met a "very cool reception"; they could not rouse sufficient interest to gather a quorum in May or August. The council for their part defended their policy competently on most points in a despatch to Whitehall. Lord Hillsborough, judging the whole affair a tempest in a teapot, seized on the absence of proofs as an excuse to ignore it and confined his remarks to a rebuke for the assembly's appeal to the people instead of to the Crown.[25] His successor, Lord Dartmouth, refused to take any

required on urgent public business; but all had been declared openly and nothing had been paid out without a previous taxing of the bills. If the creditors of the public waited, that was the fault of the assembly for not providing the money. The bill about the receiver-general had been disallowed by the Board of Trade. The building of the jail had been delayed because no contractor could be found. The pilots had refused to serve under the assembly's bill and had obtained the governor's veto. The governor's fees on whales were only £80 in seven years and none had been paid in the last two years. The laws about fisheries had been suspended merely to prevent some poor people from starving. Bruere had discharged no one from the jail; a judge of the King's Bench, Dan Lammit, had released a man in 1765 who had been illegally committed by Thomas Dickinson, then a J. P. No reversions of crown land had been made to any particular disadvantage; no timber had been taken from school land except to repair the schools. Somerset Bridge was unimportant and unnecessary. No qualified person could be found to act as second judge.

The council's excuse for the commissioners of crown land was that they had sold the land to the highest bidders.

[25] Bruere to Hillsborough, April 22, 29 and May 11, 1772; the grievances and refutations by governor and council; Hillsborough to Bruere, July 1, 1772, and Dartmouth to Bruere, November 4, 1772. All in C. O. 37 vol. 35.

action until the assembly should have used the proper methods and channels. The members themselves, chilled by the failure of their efforts, dropped their alleged grievances and even interest in them, neglecting to meet through eight adjournments. Bruere dissolved them in January 1773, met the new assembly in February and found all quiet on the legislative front.[26]

In these years 1767 to 1772 the country members had undoubtedly a case against the coterie of the capital. By their attitude to the governor, however, they had converted a willing ally into a determined enemy. Through inexperience they had presented their grievances in sadly bungled fashion. In the end they had lost the support of the Tuckers and had fallen into a hopeless confusion over Henry Tucker, Jr., which had alienated popular sentiment and ensured their defeat. They had entirely failed to remove the men of St. Georges from the seats of the mighty. But for our purpose it is worthy of note that they had conducted their agitation in radically different fashion from that set by popular leaders on the continent like Sam Adams. Harvey and Dickinson had not stirred trouble for the sake of having trouble. At no time had they called in question the authority of Parliament or the Crown. They felt no stir at mention of the word "America"; they had no ulterior nationalist motives, no doubts about their relation to the empire. They and other Bermudians had continued strangers to the developing friction between motherland and colonists in those fateful years. Their sentiment of aloofness was no doubt confirmed by the outcome of recent difficulties about salt in the Tor-

[26] Minutes of assembly for December 15, 1772, February 15 to July 23, 1773, in C. O. 40 vol. 15.

tugas and the Turks Islands, where the home authorities had upheld Bermudians against all others.[27]

It was chiefly the practical which interested the
islanders, especially if it bore in some way on illicit
trade. In 1772 the garrison of Bermuda, a detachment of the 9th Regiment, was withdrawn from the
islands; and the departure of the last cat much em-
boldened the mice. In November of that year customs
officers seized the sloop *Molly*, suspecting a cargo of
foreign rum. The captain, Perient Trott, one of the
owners (Alex. Stockdale) and others at a convenient
opportunity boarded the vessel, forced off the officers
and put to sea while a group of inhabitants looked on
in indifference. Early in 1774 the ship *Industry* of
Limerick was stranded on the northwest rocks. The
crew and passengers were saved; but some Bermudians went on board, cut the rigging and took out the
pumps, thereby disabling the vessel. The cargo was
brought ashore and sold at public auction; and the
vessel as she lay, nine miles from land, was bought
by some merchants of the island. These then procured pumps, carried them out, emptied the ship,
floated her off and brought her into port as their own
property.[28] These instances of defiance and sharp
practice showed clearly the weakness of government
on Bermuda at the approach of the American revolution.

[27] Hillsborough to Governor Shirley in the Bahamas, October 12, 1768, in
C. O. 23 vol. 17; to Lords of Admiralty, June 29, 1769, in C. O. 37 vol. 33.
[28] Bruere to Dartmouth, December 5, 1772, in C. O. 37 vol. 21 and April
19, 1774 and January 24, 1775, in C. O. 37 vol. 36.

CHAPTER III

BERMUDA AND THE CONTINENTAL CONGRESS

UNTIL 1775 the islanders had only a spectator's interest in events on the continent. Not being recipients of the East India Company's tea, they had no occasion to quarrel with the mother country over that commodity. The coercive acts which evoked sympathy for Boston from Montreal to Savannah left most Bermudians lukewarm at the best. In the autumn of 1774 the first Continental Congress declared an embargo on trade with Britain and the loyalist colonies, to take effect on September 10, 1775. This measure would of necessity affect Bermuda seriously; but most of the islanders paid little heed, feeling sure that the mother country would "pursue conciliatory measures which I believe is the ardent wish of every true lover of his country."[1] In these circumstances the desire for secession which animated the radicals of the continent stirred no spark in Bermuda.

The Tuckers, better informed of political affairs and prompted by their relatives on the continent, took a keen interest in the controversy from the time of the arrival of the tea; and, supposing that the chief object of the British ministry was "the subjecting the Americans to taxes imposed by the British Parliament" gave the colonists their entire sympathy. In this sentiment Henry of Somerset was most forward. He found fault with the violent action of the Bostonians in respect of the tea; and he recommended instead

[1] John Esten to St. George Tucker, April 3, 1775. T. H. P.

a total abstention from articles subject to tax, after the example of the Virginians. In October 1774 and again in March and May 1775, he was "big with impatience" to hear the decisions of Congress and strongly incensed at the New Yorkers for their supposed apathy.[2] His father-in-law was more reserved, consoling himself with the belief that it was not for the interest of either British or Americans to come to extremities. Nevertheless he maintained that if the ministry should persevere, the colonies ought to hazard everything rather than submit to "slavery." In the sense of the time he was a strong "Whig" although no separatist. "I shall always be of opinion that it is for the interest of both countries to be in union,"[3] he wrote later.

But Colonel Henry's sympathy with the mainland colonies was mingled with concern for Bermuda. As early as July 1774 he had been considering the prospect of an American embargo and the fatal effect of such a measure on Bermudian trade; and he cast about for some method of securing exemption for his island if the Americans should carry out their policy. Knowing that Congress would enquire why the Bermudians had not cast in their lot with the mainland, he planned to make excuse on the score of their insignificance and their utter powerlessness before the British navy and on that ground to plead for special privileges for islanders. In March 1775 he had so far formed his plans as to ask St. George to use any influence he had with the Virginia delegates to that

[2] Henry Tucker of Somerset to St. George, April 16, 1774, October 30, 1774, March 6 to May 6, 1775. T. H. P. George Forbes imagined that the coercive acts would establish an inquisition like that of Spain and Portugal, and drive millions of Americans to despair or in a manner compel them to draw their swords. To St. George Tucker, July 31, 1774, in T. H. P.

[3] Henry Tucker, Sr., to St. George, July 31, 1774 and May 8, 1778. T. H. P.

end. St. George was to make it plain that Bermudians could not identify themselves with the continent though they wished well to the Americans and that they were willing to pay for the right to import provisions by supplying America with salt and by submitting to any restraint Congress might desire to lay on their trade with the West Indies. At the same time Colonel Henry warned his son not to interest himself too far in American politics and suggested that he return home.[4] Thus unconsciously he revealed his feeling that Bermudians ought to maintain a proper distance between themselves and Americans who travelled dangerous ways.

St. George was indeed making no secret of his sympathy with the Americans; and his brother Thomas Tudor in Charleston espoused the same cause. This tendency of the sons as well as the sentiments of the father soon provoked friction between Tuckers and Brueres. George Bruere called St. George "a mere rebel" and Governor Bruere applied the term to Americans at large. Colonel Henry made excuse for his sons and their associates. The consequence was an irreparable breach between the families; "these proud spirits separated, never to meet again in friendly hall."[5] Henry Tucker, Jr., alone, concealing mild American sympathies, by an exercise of extraordinary dexterity managed to maintain friendly relations with all. Through the defection of the other Tuckers, the governor lost the chief support of his administration during the last four years. Tuckers, Bascomes, Harveys, Jennings and other principal families of the island forgot recent differences, closed ranks and from that time determined

[4] Henry Tucker, Sr., to St. George, March 6 and 26, 1775. T. H. P. St. George returned to Bermuda in June 1775.   [5] Kaye, pp. 7-8.

the policy of the legislature and to a great degree that of the islanders at large throughout the years of the American revolution.

Their first problem was to fix the direction of that policy in view of the imminence of hostilities in New England in the spring of 1775. The existing system of empire which permitted Bermudians to trade freely with the British West Indies and the colonies of the continent suited them exactly. A close calculation of economic interests then would have indicated support of the mother country against the seceding Americans as the proper course. But in the first years of the revolution no Bermudian thought that secession was the issue. In July 1777 Colonel Henry declared that he would like neither British nor Americans to obtain an advantage, which would make them think of peace. In April 1778 he caught eagerly at a rumor that Chatham would form a ministry and repeal the obnoxious acts "as I think an union much to be preferred to independency"; he wished the Americans might be of the same opinion and he imagined the chief difficulty would be the debt they had contracted.[6] Apparently in 1775 Bermudians considered the dispute a temporary matter to be composed shortly when the British ministry should abandon its claim to tax the colonists. Accordingly the thing for Bermudians to do was to keep clear of the conflict, preserve their trade and for that reason to cultivate good relations with the Americans even at the risk of giving Great Britain a little offense. Therefore the block of dominant families adopted Henry Tucker's policy of an appeal to the good nature of Congress.[7]

[6] Henry Tucker, Sr., to St. George, July 21, 1777, and April 23, 1778. T. H. P.

[7] The personnel of this block is fairly represented by the signatories of a

In May 1775 they issued invitations for a general meeting in Paget with the ostensible object of discussing the problem of food. In response some at least from each of eight parishes assembled in Paget, but only three or four men from Pembroke and none at all from Devonshire. At the meeting the Tucker group proposed election of delegates to petition the Continental Congress for exemption from its embargo as the only means of averting starvation. The suggestion surprised a good many who nevertheless having "no courage to protest nor presence of mind to foresee the ill consequence of such proceedings" held their peace.[8] The Tuckers and their friends had their own way, probably soothing the people by giving assurances that such action would mean no breach of loyalty. An address was prepared and a delegation chosen, its chairman being naturally Colonel Henry Tucker, author of the policy. The next step was to give a pledge to Congress and at the same time to assure stocks of food in Bermuda until the outcome of the negotiations could be known. Both objects would be served by an embargo on the export of provisions from the islands which would assure the Americans against any traffic to the West Indies in the commodities they might allow Bermuda. The leaders accordingly requested Bruere to summon the assembly. That body had already met at the beginning of May; and Henry Tucker of Somerset had observed

petition to Congress of March 28, 1779. They are: John Harvey, Henry Tucker (Sr.), Joseph Gilbert, John Gilbert, Jr., John Tucker, Richard Jennings, John Jennings, Robert Davenport, Edward Parker, Benjamin Bascome, Sam Harvey, Daniel Bascome, Thomas Dickinson, James Tucker, Cornelius Hinson, Thomas Nusum (Newsome?), George Robinson, Thomas Dill, Joseph Hill, John Dill. One should add Henry Tucker of Somerset and George Bascome, both of whom were very wary of signing their names. Papers of the Continental Congress 41, vol. I, folios 176-7.

[8] The Rev. T. Lyttleton to Dartmouth, undated 1775, in C. O. 37 vol. 36.

traditional amenities by finding fault with a reference in the governor's message to the controversy over the receiver-general. It had been shortly adjourned; but Bruere consented to another meeting, which took place from the 17th to the 19th. The assembly promptly passed a bill providing for an embargo of a year's duration, and fixing prices of sale. Bruere made objections, urging Lord Dunmore's assurance that Bermudians need fear no starvation if they remained loyal; but soon in face of a united front by council and assembly, he accepted the measure. By it several vessels from South Carolina laden with rice for the West Indies were laid up in harbor; and others as they arrived were also impounded. Supplies were thus assured although barely enough of Indian corn, the common food of poorer Bermudians and negroes. The legislature appointed a committee to supervise the execution of the act, including in the membership Henry Tucker of Somerset and George Bascome the clever lawyer of St. Georges. Preliminaries thus completed, the delegation set sail to Philadelphia toward the end of June or the beginning of July.[9]

Meanwhile the appeal to a rebel body had caused much uneasiness in the center parishes. Pembroke held a full meeting of its inhabitants and in a petition to the legislature expressly repudiated such dallying with sedition. "Whereas certain persons have taken upon them to represent this parish in a certain meeting in Paget's tribe, we the subscribers do assert that they were not sent by us and that we entirely disapprove of their measures and proceedings." All

[9] Minutes of assembly, May 5, 17 to 19, 1775, in C. O. 40 vol. 20. Williams, pp. 86-7. Henry Tucker, Sr., to St. George, May 29, 1775; Bascome was "punctual and diligent and has a good deal of merit" in the view of Eliza Tucker. To St. George March 6-May 6, 1775. T. H. P.

the men of Pembroke signed except the three or four who had attended the meeting. Devonshire parish adjoining, inspired by the Rev. T. Lyttleton, petitioned the legislature to address His Majesty rather than a rebel Congress about their troubles. The clergyman advised the assembly directly to the same effect without result. Mr. Thomas Burch, uncle to the chief justice, Mr. Ben Williams, justice of Devonshire and Captain Miller Cox of the same parish worked actively in the loyalist cause. Lyttleton informed Lord Dartmouth that if the fears of scarcity were removed by some plan of supply and a small force sent to protect the island against North American vessels, "the major part of the inhabitants in all probability will soon change their sentiments and the whole island remain in great quietness."[10] He was doubtless well informed about the views of the humbler inhabitants especially of the interior; and it may be stated that the first impulse of the generality of Bermudians in this summer of 1775 favored loyalty to the empire. But in midsummer it was clear that hope of an immediate reconciliation was in vain; and Bermudians were in great confusion, their livelihood endangered by both combatants but especially by the powerful navy of the motherland. Governor Bruere, hitherto unperturbed, felt a sudden change in the political atmosphere. At the end of July he was writing "there may be but few friends to government here. . . . I can't confide in any person here at present; they say they may have their vessels burnt."[11] He tried to convoke the legislature; but three times the assemblymen refused, professing a desire to wait until they had heard from Philadelphia.

[10] The Rev. T. Lyttleton to Dartmouth, undated 1775, in C. O. 37 vol. 36.
[11] Bruere to Dartmouth, July 31, 1775, in C. O. 37 vol. 36.

The delegation reached that city in July; and on the 11th Colonel Henry Tucker presented its address to Congress. He sought to make a good impression by praise of "the characters of men distinguished at this important period by the appointment of their American brethren"; and hinted at his purpose in the hope "that the utmost tenderness in your proceedings will be exercised toward such of your fellow-subjects as shall from their situation be involved in particular distress." He endeavored to show from a review of economic conditions how ill Bermuda would fare under an embargo; sought to win favor by declaring Bermudian admiration for "the noble stand made by her patriotic sons for the liberties of America" and devoutly wished that the sons of Britain would display their usual "virtue and nobleness of sentiment" by standing forth "in support of national liberty." It was still safe to throw the blame for repressive policies on ministers while exempting the King; and Henry went on to express the sentiments of his islanders. "The inhabitants of Bermuda have always been and still are desirous of proving on every occasion the most zealous attachment to His present Majesty, his crown and family." He endeavored to anticipate American demands for active support by stressing Bermudian insignificance. "Their consequence in the politics of America is too trifling for them publicly to interfere . . . they may suffer much from the contest but their utmost exertion can contribute nothing to the support of it." In conclusion he prayed for adoption of some method to secure provisions for the islanders if the embargo should actually come into force; and he entreated divine intervention to restore peace and harmony to the whole

British Empire on satisfactory constitutional principles.[12]

Congress, however, was in a mood to give Bermuda exactly nothing for nothing and so it probably informed the delegates. But it was ready to throw out a broad hint about terms of a possible agreement. It asked for statistics of provisions imported into Bermuda for some years past and it communicated a recent decision that the embargo on exports would not apply to vessels bringing arms or powder in exchange. Presently it emphasized the point by a resolution of August 1, 1775, defining the islands and colonies included in the embargo and mentioning Bermuda specifically.[13] These actions brought to the fore the question of powder. For a long time some 112 barrels of that commodity had lain unguarded in the royal magazine of St. Georges, intended of course for the use of the King's troops against his enemies. But now enterprising rebels had in mind to use it against the King's troops. A Bermudian named Harris was discussing the matter with Washington at Cambridge, and offering to guide an expedition for a price.[14] Thomas Tudor Tucker was urging the committee of safety at Charleston to possess itself of the valuable explosive; and St. George Tucker, before returning to Bermuda in June 1775, mentioned the powder to Peyton Randolph, then president of Congress, and perhaps to Thomas Jefferson also.[15] It was probably

[12] To the honorable the delegates of the confederated American colonies from Nova Scotia to Georgia assembled in Congress at Philadelphia. The address of deputies from the different parishes of the islands of Bermuda. T. H. P.

[13] Journals of the Continental Congress, II, 174, 187, 239. Edited by W. C. Ford. Washington; Government Printing Office, 1905.

[14] P. Force, American Archives, fourth series, III, 36 (Washington to Governor Nicholas Cooke, August 4, 1775).

[15] St. George Tucker to Richard Rush, October 27, 1813. *Virginia Magazine*

these two who inspired the reply of Congress to the Bermudian address. At any rate Congress handed the affair over to the Pennsylvania committee of safety on which sat Ben Franklin and Robert Morris; and Franklin undertook the negotiations with the islanders. Colonel Henry Tucker was in a difficult position. He had not come to Philadelphia to aid the King's enemies; he had thought himself a loyal subject of the King and had so informed Congress. Now he must either abandon his mission or perform the most disloyal of acts. The interests of Bermuda, as he saw them, guided his decision; and he made arrangements with Franklin to trade the powder of St. Georges for an exemption from the embargo. He was back in Bermuda by July 25. The Pennsylvania committee of safety engaged the sloop *Lady Catherine*, Captain George Ord master, with forty picked men, and sent her after the delegation. At the same time Thomas Tudor Tucker's advice took effect in Charleston; and the committee of safety of that place sent the schooner *Charleston and Savannah Packet* on the same errand. It reached Bermuda early in August; but the crew saw no immediate opportunity of carrying out their purpose and cleared from St. Georges on the 11th. Nevertheless they hung around the island for a turn of fortune, perhaps on the suggestion of the Tuckers.

In the meantime in July, Henry Tucker of Somerset had obtained a consignment of eight half barrels of powder. Unlike his father-in-law, he was troubled by no hauntings of loyalty; he intended to use this powder for the benefit of the Americans in arms and his own pocket. He discussed with St. George a pro-

of History and Biography, July 1934, pp. 211-21, edited by Mrs. G. P. Coleman of Tucker House, Williamsburg.

ject for selling it in Virginia; then, finding Copeland
Stiles arrived from Philadelphia, endeavored to learn
the prospects of a market in that city. But Stiles had
no better suggestion than to send the powder to
South Carolina.[16] The returning delegation, however,
had the solution for Henry's problem as part of its
own. They selected a committee to execute their plans,
including George Bascome, Nathaniel Todd and
Stephen Judkin; Henry Tucker, Sr., of course being
chairman. At the beginning of August a letter from
Franklin arrived, brought by Captain Trimingham,
to the effect that Congress was inclined to assist the
Bermudians but had not yet formed a plan to prevent
them from reexporting provisions to the West Indies.[17]
At this juncture Captain Ord arrived with the *Lady
Catherine*, put in at the west end and anchored near
the entrance to Mangrove Bay.

Colonel Henry Tucker, Henry of Somerset and
Richard Jennings met him and made their plans.
Henry of Somerset took charge, being the ideal man
for such a business. He wanted some light sailboats
and on August 14 sent his henchman and relative
James Tucker of Paget to ask Joseph Jennings at the
Flats for his boats and men, professedly on behalf of
Richard, making no secret of the purpose. Joseph
Jennings being in some degree a loyalist, refused and
urged James Tucker to inform the governor, which
he in his turn of course refused.[18] But other islanders
were not so scrupulous as Joseph Jennings, and furnished Henry all the conveyances and assistance he
desired. The plotters doubtless informed St. George
Tucker but did not require of him any active assist-

[16] Henry Tucker of Somerset to St. George, July 29, 1775. T. H. P.
[17] Henry Tucker, Sr., to St. George, August 6, 1775. T. H. P.
[18] Henry Tucker, Sr., to St. George, April 19, 1786. T. H. P.

ance; and he was walking on the parade with the chief justice that evening until nearly midnight. At that time Ord's crew and a few Bermudian west enders guided by Henry of Somerset proceeded in sailboats from Mangrove Bay eastward along the north side. They soon landed near the naval tanks of St. Georges and marched to the magazine on Retreat Hill just east of Government House. They found the magazine as usual without semblance of a guard, broke through the top and let a man down who forced the doors. Entry secured, they seized the barrels and rolled them to the beach, some actually through Government House grounds. The approach of dawn perhaps prevented a complete clearance of the magazine; but by that time the band had loaded one hundred barrels on their boats and were returning westward. They were discovered by an old resident who called his son and told him that the deed would be a dark cloud hanging over Bermuda. The reputation of Bermuda, however, was of no importance to the raiders, who speedily placed their plunder on the *Packet* and the *Lady Catherine*, taking Henry of Somerset's eight half barrels on the latter vessel.[19] The ships were soon on their way to the continent. Captain George Ord reached Philadelphia by August 26 with a letter from Colonel Henry to the Pennsylvania committee of safety and some 1800 pounds of powder, part of which had spoiled, leaving 1182 pounds usable worth £161 14s. 18d., Bermuda currency. Robert Morris entered an account of the importation on his committee's books and respecting

[19] St. George Tucker to Richard Rush, October 27, 1813, cited above; Delancey Cleveland in *Evening Post*, New York, February 24, 1904. Mr. Cleveland had access to the papers of Ord but errs in the name of Ord's vessels.

Henry of Somerset's desire to remain modestly
anonymous, credited the eight half barrels to Captain
John Cowper of North Carolina, Henry's agent on
the continent.[20] The *Packet* reached Charleston in
safety also and deposited her powder, which served
the guns of Fort Moultrie against the attack by Sir
Peter Parker.[21] Colonel Henry Tucker had well fulfilled his part of the contract with Congress.

Meanwhile in the morning of the 15th of August,
Bruere learned of the theft, saw the *Lady Catherine*
in the distance and realized in horror that the powder
was being conveyed away for the use of subjects in
arms against the King. He issued a proclamation
hastily worded. "Save your country from ruin which
may hereafter happen! The powder stole out of the
magazine late last night cannot be carried far as the
wind is so light. A great reward will be given to any
person that can make a proper discovery before the
magistrates." He called the council and induced it to
order magistrates of parishes to do all in their power
to detect the persons concerned in "the atrocious
act" and the customs officers to search all vessels out-
ward bound.[22] He succeeded in convoking the legislature on the 16th. Most of the members of the assembly
must have been cognizant of, and a few like Henry
Tucker of Somerset privy to, the theft or active in it;
and they thought it politic to make a gesture which
would keep their official characters clear without

[20] Colonial Records of Pennsylvania, X, 321, 341. Harrisburg, 1852.
[21] St. George Tucker to Richard Rush, October 27, 1813, cited above.
The part of Henry of Somerset in the actual theft is inferred from George
Bruere's reference to him as generally suspected of being the "chief promoter
of the powder robbery." (To Ben. Thompson, October 19, 1781, in C. O. 37
vol. 38.) The interpretation falls short of entire certainty but seems most
likely in view of all the evidence.
[22] Minutes of executive council, August 15, 1775. (Bermuda Archives.)

bringing a discovery. They voted a reward of £100 to the finder of the perpetrators, Bruere offering pardon and an additional £30 to anyone who would turn King's evidence. Pardon and reward alike remained unclaimed; "the minds of the people are very much poisoned since they chose delegates" the governor confessed sadly.[23]

His next recourse was to send a report of his troubles to General Thomas Gage in Boston. He had already an intimate link with Gage's army in that two of his sons had served in it as lieutenants, one of whom (John Bruere) had been killed at Bunker. He now endeavored to charter a vessel to carry despatches to Boston, and had secured a sloop when the owner received threats that the rudder and sail would be removed if he offered to fit her. Bruere took the matter to council and enquired for a substitute vessel. Chief Justice Burch had one which was for hire but was out of repair and had neither master nor men. No other councillor owned a vessel or knew of one to be hired in a whole community of seafarers; they were doubtless the victims of artificial ignorance. Bruere made shift for himself, increased his offer to £50 and by September 3 succeeded in persuading an owner to undertake the service. Just as the sloop was getting under sail, the mate refused to go. The governor, not to be balked, procured a negro to complete the crew and sent a slave of his own on board with the

[23] Bruere to Dartmouth, August 17, 1775, in C. O. 37 vol. 36; minutes of assembly, August 16, 1775, in C. O. 40 vol. 20. The rest of the powder, about twelve barrels, was removed to the top room of the court house which had been the store room for powder for nearly one hundred years before the magazine had been built. The townsmen of St. Georges feared fire and protested. Bruere then repaired the magazine and on advice of council put the powder back in it under care of a watch. Minutes of executive council, August 31, 1775. Bermuda Archives.

despatches; and he arranged with the captain that at a signal fire the vessel should hasten away. The captain then put to sea with a crew of three negroes and lay outside the harbor waiting for a wind. Word of his intention had meanwhile reached the Tuckers. Henry of Somerset, who had probably been at the bottom of the governor's trouble over sloops, and two or three members of the assembly gathered a band of sixteen or eighteen and put out in the direction of the vessel, giving out that she had rice or flour on board which they as men of the legislature's committee on such matters were bound to detain. Bruere, on the hill looking to the sloop, became aware of the pursuit and lit his signal fire. It was too late; the party caught the sloop. Four or five white men boarded her and asked the captain for the letters he carried. He replied that he had none, doubtless allaying any qualms of conscience by the thought that the documents were in possession of the slave securely hidden below. The party, failing to find the letters, beat and abused the captain; and presently, fearing the rising wind, returned to St. Georges at one in the morning. The captain set sail and in good time reached Boston with the despatches.[24] Gage and Admiral Howe took prompt heed of the cry for help and sent the *Scorpion* with a transport of six hundred tons to Bermuda for a stay of six weeks. Bruere still had thirty pieces of ordnance, of little value when the stock of powder was reduced to a dozen barrels. In mid-October he learned that another American vessel was hovering about the coast and took alarm lest she intended to fetch the ordnance after the one hundred barrels of powder.

[24] Bruere to Dartmouth, August 20, September 2 and 13, 1775, February 23, 1776 in C. O. 37 vol. 36; minutes of executive council August 31, 1775, Bermuda Archives.

He persuaded Captain Tollemache of the *Scorpion* to take the precious cannon on board and carry them away at his departure. Thus Bermuda was left without defenses of any sort.[24a]

By this time the Continental Congress was ready to consider the affairs of Bermuda. Colonel Henry Tucker made up the required statistics on Bermudian imports for the previous three years with an estimate for the next; and these he despatched to Congress for its session of September 13, increasing the population of the islands from 10,000 to 15,000 to be on the safe side. In face of his practical and convincing response to the request for powder, Congress could not remain indifferent. On October 2 a committee reported in favor of export to Bermuda, payment to be made in salt or other commodities not tainted by a British origin, except tea.[25] After full consideration, on November 22 Congress resolved "that the inhabitants of the island of Bermuda appear friendly to the cause of America" and ought to obtain supplies necessary for their subsistence and home consumption, on condition of repayment in salt, arms or ammunition. The amount of provisions was set at 72,000 bushels of Indian corn, 2000 barrels of bread or flour, 1000 of beef or pork, 2100 bushels of peas or beans and 300 terces of rice, the business of supply to be shared among the Carolinas, Virginia, Maryland, Pennsylvania and New York. Congress in generous mood added that it would permit export of other necessaries such as lumber, soap and candles whenever the quantity and quality of Bermudian needs were ascertained; and it arranged for the immediate supply of

[24a] The ordnance business in Bruere to Dartmouth, October 16, 1775 in C.O. 37 vol. 36 and minutes of executive council October 10, 11, 1775.
[25] Journals of the Continental Congress, II, 246, III, 268.

islanders by authorizing Mr. Edward Stiles of Pennsylvania (a former Bermudian) to send the brig *Sea Nymph*, Sam Stobel master, to Bermuda at once with a cargo. In the middle of next summer (July 24, 1776) Congress reaffirmed its resolutions on embargo and confiscation and again explicitly excepted Bermuda and the Bahamas. And in November 1777 it exempted Bermudian vessels from capture by American privateers and inserted the exemption from that time in letters of marque.[26] So was signed and sealed the alliance of Congress with the block of dominant families in Bermuda which remained for these the basis of policy until 1782 although it came officially to an end in 1781.

So also commenced or continued an extensive business between continentals and Bermudian mariners which represented to the latter the most important fact about the war. Echoes of it occasionally reached Congress; for instance, in May 1776 the men of Greenwich in Cumberland County, New Jersey, reported that the sloop *Betsey and Ann*, Ben Tucker master, had arrived from Bermuda and desired to exchange 1700 bushels of salt and two puncheons of rum for provisions. Congress gave the required permission on the understanding that Mr. Tucker would proceed direct to Bermuda and do his best to avoid English cutters or men of war.[27] In asking for permission, the men of Greenwich and Mr. Tucker were paying excessive deference to formalities; for certainly most of the trade never came to the official knowledge of Congress. In 1775-1776 some islanders procured

[26] Journals of the Continental Congress, III, 362-5, V, 606. Verrill, pp. 51, 57, 62. The Bahamas were included for the sake of the salt on Turks Islands, not for the attitude of the inhabitants who remained loyal in great majority.
[27] Journals, V, 417.

small quantities of powder, perhaps from neutral colonies, brought it in their sloops to the middle harbors of Bermuda and sent it off when accumulated to the Americans. Twenty sail of Bermuda vessels, nominally engaged in picking up wrecks and turtles at the Bahama banks, sold the revolting colonists ships, salt, cannon and military stores, thus keeping in supplies the American privateers who preyed on the West India trade. In fact, most American privateering ships were Bermuda-built. The salt makers at Turks Islands did a lively trade, exchanging their product for flour and grain.[28] Of this business the Tuckers endeavored strenuously to secure their part. In the summer of 1776 St. George Tucker, having failed to secure for himself Attorney-General Hunt's position, and seeing the law silent in the clash of arms, turned to commerce for a livelihood.[29] He and two or three others, presumably including his father, bought a sloop entitled *Dispatch* and shared in the smuggling of rice until that commodity became a drug on the market.[30] In November he decided to return to the continent; he cleared with his vessel for the West Indies but went to Turks Islands, loaded with salt and proceeded to Virginia where grateful state authorities bought his cargo at a good price.[31] He now became continental agent and manager for the family in various enterprises. He employed the *Dispatch*, bought another vessel the *Adelphi* on family account and engaged others as occasion arose. The *Dispatch* made one or two voyages into the West

[28] George Bruere to Germain, August 7, 1776, in C. O. 37 vol. 36.
[29] On the attorney-generalship, Eliza Tucker to St. George, March 6 to May 6, 1775, in T. H. P.
[30] Henry Tucker, Jr., to St. George, June 18, 1776. T. H. P.
[31] St. George Tucker to Richard Rush, cited above. He also traded indigo for arms in the West Indies, using four vessels.

Indies which returned profit enough to enable St.
George to live in fair comfort; but other ventures
were not so successful. He sent a brig for salt to
Curaçao in early 1777 with a cargo under care of his
brother Thomas Tudor Tucker; but he underesti-
mated by half the freightage charge to his consigners
and did not make enough from it to cover the insurance cost, thereby earning a reprimand from his
father. That summer St. George employed young
Thomas Tucker and his sloop on some obscure mission; both were captured but the loss this time was
covered by insurance. Another Tucker, called "old
captain," in the fall of 1777 brought 3000 bushels of
salt to North Carolina for St. George and the Colonel,
who hoped that it would sell in Virginia for £4 or £5
a bushel. The colonel gave general directions for procedure in the salt business to delude ships of war; St.
George was to use Dutch colors and to obtain clearances in Sandy Point, St. Kitts, for return to Bermuda. In 1778 St. George send the *Adonis*, Captain
Trimingham, to Curaçao with results satisfactory to
his father save that Trimingham fell into the hands
of the French on his return and had to be reclaimed.
In that year St. George apparently chartered the
Adelphi to Norton and Beale, being overreached in
the process by those two and by George Gibbs the
master; then he sold her, thereby spoiling his father's
plans for future business and earning another reprimand as the sales price was less than the original cost
of the sloop and was difficult to collect at that. The
son sent a cargo of tobacco in the *Dispatch* to Bordeaux in 1778. The port was reached and the cargo
sold but only for a sum which fell much short of old
Henry's expectations. The colonel in fact never attained more than limited confidence in his youngest

son's business ability. The outbreak of war with
France in 1778 made no difference to the *Dispatch*.
She was to repeat her voyage in 1779; but by December of that year the old man had received no word of
her or the insurance.[32] The colonel engaged in independent ventures also; in early 1777 he bought a
large American prize sloop and sent it under care of
George Gibbs with a cargo of molasses to New York,
thereby with great impartiality supplying the British
army after the Americans. He was not averse to
business even with Great Britain; in 1778 he put
£2000 of Spanish indigo on two brigs for London but
presently heard that they had fallen into the hands
of New Englanders who released them apparently on
condition that they should not continue to England.
Old Henry had three sloops in South Carolina in the
spring of 1779; but in that year he lost the *Sally Van*,
which may have been one of them. The impression
one gathers of the ventures of Colonel Henry and St.
George is one of only moderate success at best. The
old man advised his son not to give up the law; "you
will find it a more certain profit than the precarious
advantages of trade."[33]

The opportunities of contraband trade were much
too obvious to be missed by that clever person,
Henry Tucker of Somerset. In 1777 he had a quarter
share in a cargo of 3000 bushels of salt in the sloop
Success, which justified her name under Captain John
Tucker. In 1778 he sent a brig with his father-in-law's
ill-fated venture in indigo. In 1780 he had a vessel
which procured salt in Anguilla, proceeded to Nova

[32] Henry Tucker, Sr., to St. George, April 2, June 22, November 5, 1777,
October 15, 1778, April 6, 21, June 3, December 27, 1779. T. H. P.

[33] Henry Tucker, Sr., to St. George, April 2, 1777, February 24, April 21,
June 3, December 27, 1779. The quotation from letter of June 3.

Scotia for lumber and spars and was to return to Bermuda and go thence to Virginia, the cargo to be received by Wills and John Cowper of Suffolk, sometime of North Carolina. In the last years of the war he employed the brig *Friendship* which twice made the trip to St. Eustatia, St. Thomas and Turks. The record of Henry of Somerset's operations is only sketchy but definite enough of results. In December 1777 he wrote of "many other of my adventures" in Virginia and declared "I have now much at stake." In 1780 he was so crowded with business that even with several assistants he could with difficulty discharge it.[34] From the amounts owing him by Wills and John Cowper (£500 in November 1779, £800 odd in July 1780, £677 in January 1781) as well as from his purchase of a one hundred-acre farm in April we may conclude that in skill and success at contraband trade he much surpassed the other Tuckers. Many other Bermudians engaged in the business—Darrell, Trimingham, Dickinson, Prudden, Albouy, various subordinate Tuckers and Morgans with a host who kept their names out of documents. For the convenience of the trade in general, Dan Jennings settled in the Dutch island of St. Eustatia and from that haven, safe until 1780, acted as agent and financial intermediary to Bermudians in general and the Tuckers in particular.[35] So notorious did the commercial relations of Americans and Bermudians become that a British captain in the Bay of Fundy endeavored to entrap

[34] Henry Tucker of Somerset to St. George, December 17, 1777, November 27, 1779, August 17, 1780. The *Friendship* got into difficulties and settlement of her affairs with Cowper dragged on until 1786. To St. George, December 13, 1781, December 17, 1782, January 11, 1783, June 22, 1784, February 19 and April 20, 1785, April 24 and August 24, 1786. T. H. P.

[35] Henry Tucker, Sr., to St. George, September 4, 1778. T. H. P.

the American officer John Allan by passing off his vessel as a Bermudian.[36]

Good relations in business led naturally to social and diplomatic friendliness. In the autumn of 1775 General Washington induced Governor Cooke of Rhode Island to send a sloop under Captain Abraham Whipple on the same errand as Ord and the *Lady Catherine*. About mid-October Whipple put in at the west end of Bermuda. The inhabitants at first took his to be an armed vessel belonging to the King and fell into "the utmost confusion," women and children fleeing into the country. Whipple managed to show some of them his American commission and his instructions. At once they recovered from their fright and treated him with great "cordiality and friendship," informing him of the removal of the powder and the arrival of the *Scorpion*. News of his coming having spread, five of the King's council of Bermuda ventured on board his ship and assured him that the people were "hearty friends to the American cause and heartily disposed to serve it." In such a congenial atmosphere Whipple had no difficulty in obtaining the supplies he wanted for his return to the continent.[37]

It was now safe for an American envoy to visit Bermuda. In April 1776 Silas Dean on his way to France stopped in the west end and was hospitably entertained by Henry Tucker of Somerset and to a minor degree by Colonel Henry. Dean soon conceived an opinion "the people in this island are zealous in the American cause and appear willing to do every-

[36] John Allan to Jeremiah Powell, August 9, 1778 (Archives of Massachusetts, vol. 144, pp. 241-4).

[37] American Archives, fourth series, III, 1181-2. (Cooke to Washington, October 25, 1775.)

thing in their power to promote it." The natives offered him, at a price, privateers and guns to match, four to nine pounders surviving from the Seven Years War; and explained that they had already sold the Americans some of these pieces. Mr. John Jennings the assemblyman had a fine ship on the stocks of eighty-foot keel which he was anxious to sell, equipped with guns if necessary. Dean's Bermudian friends filled his ears with tales of dire distress about to overtake the island, and urged the necessity of more aid from Congress. In the face of such evident sympathy, he advised Congress to seize and fortify the islands as a base for intercepting British trade with the West Indies. "The inhabitants, I am confident, would receive you as their best friends." Congress, however, had not the resources to undertake such an expedition, although from time to time it entertained the idea. Dean found it easy to hire a fast sloop, the *Mary*, with which he soon reached Bordeaux.[38]

Perhaps through his representations, Henry Tucker of Somerset was unofficially nominated as philosopher and friend to American mariners visiting Bermuda. By October 1777 it was arranged that American vessels falling in with the Bermudas would stand for the west end and hoist a jack at the maintop masthead. At this signal a Mr. Tucker, evidently Henry, would give them assistance, orders or information. It is not certain, however, that he retained this position long. In December 1777 the American brig, *Commerce*

[38] Silas Dean to Congress, April 26, 1776, in American Archives, fourth series, V, 1083-5. Lafayette wrote to Vergennes, July 3 and 18, 1779, about the possibility of seizing Bermuda for the Americans; and on February 2, 1780, he spoke of touching in at Bermuda to establish the party of liberty there. (Verrill, p. 61.) In the T. H. P. there is a copy of a contract for the *Mary* between Dean on one hand and the Jennings and J. Morgan on the other.

buffeted by storms on a trip from Nantes, put in at Somerset, Bermuda; and her captain applied to Henry Tucker, understanding him to be an agent for Congress. Henry advised him to unload and strip her and put everything into his hands. When this had been done, Collector Smith's men arrived at the west end, seized the sloop and sent her with a cargo to London. Thereby the captain lost both vessel and goods. For Henry of Somerset, having double-dealt successfully with British officers for more than two years, was quite capable of cheating his friends the Americans if a good opportunity offered.[39] The incident, however, was nothing more than a fleeting cloud over the excellent relations between Congress and the leaders of Bermuda. The understanding, sought by the islanders in 1775 in the belief that the war was merely a temporary interruption of inter-imperial harmony, persisted even when in 1778 the issue was clearly seen to be separation, the Bermudians weighing only immediate advantages.[40] In this way the mariners, shipowners and their employees, in all the greater part of the inhabitants, came to play the rôle of allies of the United States. Most of them had no conviction on the subject, considering it a matter of business, and they had no notion of sharing the political fortunes of the States. Thus they were able better to hoodwink the positively loyal inhabitants. These may have numbered one-third of the population and were strongest in the central parishes, but finding no subversive movement to oppose, and lacking leadership until 1780, they drifted helplessly.

[39] The signal for Henry of Somerset in a manuscript in the Auckland collection, King's College, Cambridge, quoted in Verrill, p. 62; affair of the *Commerce* in Journals of the Continental Congress, XII, 105-8.

[40] Henry Tucker, Sr., to St. George, May 8, 1778. "I have my doubts and fears that what would have satisfied the Americans eighteen months ago will not do so now." T. H. P.

CHAPTER IV

BERMUDA AND HIS MAJESTY'S NAVY

THE relations of Bermuda and the United States were satisfactory enough to both parties but not to a third. For Great Britain, sovereign of Bermuda, was at war with the same United States; and though inclined to be long-suffering, would not indefinitely tolerate the giving of aid and comfort to her enemy. In November 1775, Parliament passed an act for prohibition of trade and intercourse with the thirteen colonies. Thereafter the price for the convenience of such intercourse was likely to be the inconvenience of a supervision by His Majesty's navy. Yet that navy was busy on the North American coasts and might not give more than perfunctory attention to the vagaries of islanders in mid-Atlantic. It seemed to leading Bermudians that the risk was worth running.

The navy was indeed well occupied with American vessels and coast defenses in 1775-1776 and reluctant to disperse itself for the sake of apparently insignificant islands. It was accordingly not a question of contraband that first brought a warship to Bermuda but as we have seen, the theft of the powder which was a real act of rebellion. The *Scorpion* remained until her commander was confident that there would be no rising to suppress; and in the interval she came into conflict with the embargo passed by the legislature of Bermuda in May.

That embargo had soon evoked protests and petitions from the owners of detained vessels who had cargoes for Antigua or Dominica and were now hindered in their business and prevented from succoring the loyal Leeward Islanders. Bruere could not but heed the plea and he called the assembly to consider it. That body replied that they would take no action until the result of the appeal to Congress should be known. The assurances of the Tuckers after the robbery of the magazine probably led them to expect a favorable answer. In the session of mid-August they suspended part of the embargo until September 10 to permit export of rice which was the property of non-Bermudians only. Bruere, failing to obtain any discretionary power for himself, acquiesced, excusing himself to the home authorities by the needs of Antigua and Dominica. The embargo had thus resumed its force when the *Scorpion* arrived in mid-September, frightening off the provision vessels from the continent and prepared to treat the islanders as rebels. These sought an opportunity to retaliate in their own way and presently found it.

The captain desired to purchase supplies and heard of stores of rice at the west end. In the evening of September 28 he sent a shallop with a party of men under Lieutenant Drew from St. Georges. The news rapidly spread to the west; and the local leaders determined to prevent the purchase in order the sooner to get rid of the *Scorpion*. They went on a schooner just arrived from Charleston with rice and removed her sails, boom and rudder. Another party repaired to Bethell's island to secure a warehouse stocked with rice, bread and flour. Presently the shallop arrived. Lieutenant Drew asked the captain of the schooner for permission to buy the rice; the captain, instructed by the local worthies, refused. These, Richard and John Jennings and Dan Tucker asked the officer the reason for his visit. He replied politely that he had come merely to buy provisions for government account. They declared that any export of provisions was contrary to law; he stated that he knew nothing of the law and was acting under orders. Finally they conceived it desirable to avoid responsibility and said that a passenger named Cole if anyone had power to sell.[1] Thereupon the company dispersed save for a few who kept watch. The sailors remained at the west end for the night. In the morning Drew made another attempt to carry out his mission, came on board the schooner and asked for Cole. This person responded but declared that the rice was owned in St. Kitts and was not for sale. The officer now tried a threat; he demanded the sails and told the captain he had orders to take the vessel to customs in town. At this point the local men on guard, Robert Tucker, Dan Hinson, Josiah Young, came on board and refused to permit the vessel or the rice to be moved. The officer departed, threatening to bring the whole force of the *Scorpion*. The local men replied that they would use force to repel attacks on property or breaches of the law; and they took the rice on shore.

Captain Tollemache, informed by Drew, sent a letter of remonstration to Richard Fowler and Daniel Bell, justices of Somerset and Port Royal. These two referred the matter to local committees representative of the Gilberts, Jennings and especially of the Tuckers, Colonel Henry, Henry of Somerset and St. George all being members. It was the nimble brain of the second which planned the strategy of the reply; a declaration of the strictest allegiance to His Majesty and abhorrence of any attempt to oppose legal authority, an emphasis on the necessity of measures to avoid famine, an appeal, repeated in a separate com-

[1] Bruere to Germain, April 19, 1777, C. O. 37 vol. 36; unsigned letter to St. George Tucker, September 29, 1775, in T. H. P.

munication to the governor, for the convocation of the legislature as the only body fit to deal with the question of rice.[2] Thus Henry threw the dust of loyal phrases into the eyes of the captain and the loyal inhabitants. He was endeavoring also to trick the governor into calling a session of the assembly in which he would find opportunities to embarrass governor and warship alike. But Bruere was not so easily taken in; he ignored the petition and prevented the session, due shortly by another adjournment. The west enders might consider strict legality in transactions with His Majesty's navy, but allowed a certain tempering on other occasions; and when Whipple arrived, they supplied him freely in oblivion of the embargo. Toward the end of October the *Scorpion* went from Bermuda and left the islanders free to do business with the continent. Soon provisions were plentiful and cheap.[2a]

In the spring, however, the British navy established a better blockade of the American coast and for a time almost stifled this business, 120 vessels being compelled to lie in harbor at Bermuda when Silas Dean arrived. Early in April Bruere managed to despatch a sloop with a cargo of supplies to General Howe, by manning it with his own house negroes; thereby for the second time he outwitted his islanders.[3] By this time the stocks of provisions were running low except for two or three thousand bushels of wheat which had a slow sale, the islanders pre-

[2] Henry of Somerset to St. George, undated but of October 1775, with various enclosed papers and minutes of evidence regarding this affair in T.H.P. Daniel Bell may be the same person as Nathaniel Bell, p. 72.

[2a] *Independent Chronicle*, March 13, 1777.

[3] Bruere to Germain, April 14, 1776, in C. O. 37 vol. 36. He had dissolved the assembly on February 22, 1776, and held elections which made little difference to the membership.

ferring Indian corn for their negroes. The merchants of St. Georges desired to export the wheat and take advantage of rising prices, for which they needed and would undoubtedly receive the assembly's consent. Bruere baffled them by repeated adjournments, gaining the thanks of many who preferred the grain to the profits of the grain trade. In May the wheat was disposed of, and at the same time the embargo act expired. At the end of June Bruere called the legislature which passed a bill to renew the prohibition of export. But the governor had in the meantime caught a suspicion that the new colonial secretary Lord George Germain disliked the embargo as an injury to the loyal colonies of the West Indies. He delayed the bill for a week, then vetoed it; and shortly received confirmation of his course in a formal notification that His Majesty disapproved of such embargoes.[4] One subject of dispute between islanders and Royal navy was thereby removed, to the advantage of the latter.

The real trial of strength, however, was about to come. Admiral Lord Howe decided on a serious effort to execute the act of November and to interrupt Bermudian business with the continent. He sent two vessels to sojourn at Bermuda in the summer of 1776, the sloop of war *Nautilus*, Captain John Collins, which arrived on June 19, and her sister the *Galatea*, Captain Thomas Jordan, which came on September 7 and remained for some time after the *Nautilus* had departed on October 20. These vessels commenced an offensive against contraband trade and soon captured several Bermudian craft who had been trading with the Americans in the West Indies or Philadel-

[4] Bruere to Dartmouth, February 23, 1776, to Germain, April 19, 1777, in C. O. 37 vol. 36. Minutes of executive council, July 10, 1776. (Bermuda Archives.)

phia. When the *Nautilus* brought her first prize into the admiralty court of St. Georges, she encountered an obstacle; John Esten the judge resigned, "being accustomed to trade or have connections in North America." The governor induced John Randle, deputy secretary, to accept the unpopular position, and found that his nominee refused him any share in the fees. The business of hunting illicit traders went on actively in spite of this minor difficulty, the last episode of the year being the capture of Jeremiah Morgan whom the *Galatea* took to New York with her in November. When she had departed, Bermudian sloops went swiftly to work with the result that by the New Year "we are happy in having a sufficient supply for many months."[5]

Early in January, however, a vessel of war appeared "so that our harvest is in all probability over." This and two others (*Galatea, Nautilus* and *Repulse*), were presently busy around Bermudian coasts, having taken eight prizes on the voyage from New York. The *Galatea* had sunk an American privateer; and on reaching Bermuda she hesitated over a sloop and let it go, her captain thinking it one from Turks Islands which he had inspected the day before. In fact the sloop was George Lusher's, carrying a notorious rebel, Thomas Tudor Tucker, home for a visit to his family. The *Repulse* soon went away but the others remained, the *Galatea* making herself particularly disliked by islanders. Lieutenant W. A. Merrick of that ship was on the hunt in charge of a boat on February 20, 1777, when he caught sight of a suspect

[5] Bruere to Germain, November 30, 1776 and April 22, 1777, C. O. 37 vol. 36; Henry Tucker, Sr., to St. George, January 5, 1777, in T. H. P. Morgan had flour and corn from Philadelphia. Resignation of Esten in minutes of executive council, July 10, 1776. (Bermuda Archives.)

sloop from the west end. He pursued his quarry among the rocks to a wharf at Salt Kettle[5a]; and the men of the sloop, run to earth, fired at the sailors. Merrick landed his men and prepared to return the fire but found that the firearms could not be discharged in the rain. He then ordered his men to draw their cutlasses and charge. In the ensuing scuffle some Bermudians were wounded but apparently none seriously. A crowd of inhabitants now assembled and adopted a menacing tone. Rather than risk a conflict, Merrick withdrew his men to the boat; and the natives carried off the cargo. Next day the lieutenant returned and burnt the sloop. Poor Bruere on learning of the incident "cautioned the inhabitants in the strongest terms not to make any resistance in future to His Majesty's officers in the execution of their duty if they are desirous to keep the peace."[6]

The naval captains had little faith in grandmotherly expostulations. Finding a difficulty in the length of Bermudian coast, in March 1777 they fitted out a schooner as tender and stationed her for some time in Ely's Harbour; and they garrisoned a dilapidated fort at Hogfish Cut. They soon discovered that Bermudian mariners could recognize a vessel of war at surprising distances and, recognizing, avoid. Lieutenant Merrick therefore commandeered a sloop and crew of slaves belonging to Thomas Tucker and kept it out cruising as a decoy for home-bound Bermudians, much to the disgust of the owner who went to law and secured from a jury a verdict of £300 odd and costs which he was quite unable to collect. The

[5a] This is a spur of land east of the Paget-Warwick boundary.
[6] Bruere to Germain, March 4 and April 19, 1777, in C. O. 37 vol. 36. Henry Tucker, Sr., to St. George, January 13, 1777. T. H. P.

decoy boat shortly took five vessels, three Americans and two Bermudians (Hutchings of Somerset and John Matholin). The natives had a reply; Hale and Dickinson's boat went out in theory to fish, in reality to warn friends about the decoy. The sailors, however, suspected the ruse, seized the boat, took her sails and sank her. Merrick caught another suspect sloop belonging to George Harvey, stripped it of its sails and burnt it. Harvey for his part took legal action and secured a verdict of £126 and costs which was quite as uncollectable as Thomas Tucker's. While the decoy was thus occupied, the two naval vessels reaped a harvest of prizes. Captain Collins took one, the property of a Bermudian named Forbes, to New York and had her condemned before the owner could put in a defense. The two commanders had no confidence in Bermudian jails or juries and kept their prisoners on board or sent them to New York, as happened to Murray and Musson. One man, Wainwright, detained on ship, secured a writ of habeas corpus from the chief justice for his release; but Captain Jordan defied that venerable safeguard of liberties and refused to give up his prisoner until the offenders at Salt Kettle should be brought in, which of course postponed the event to the Greek Kalends, Wainwright meanwhile being transferred to New York. The officers found that in spite of all their efforts some sloops slipped through and landed cargoes of contraband. Thus it became necessary to search on shore; and the sailors broke open John Harvey's stores and entered several houses by force in their pursuit of goods or deserters. Lieutenant Merrick, similarly occupied, destroyed some guns belonging to the estate of Francis Jones, late president of the council. The men of the navy soon discovered the objections of the islanders to their proceedings and stigmatized them as "rebels," even men of the "first characters" as Colonel Henry complained while Bruere wished helplessly that both captains and people would be more moderate. The *Galatea* left Bermuda in April but the *Nautilus* continued until October. Not only did these ships beset the island, but tenders from Jamaica appeared at Turks Islands and temporarily broke up the business in salt, sending several Bermudians home empty. The summer of 1777 was a hard one for Bermudian contraband.[7]

In the winter of 1777-1778 the islanders were again left alone and made the most of their breathing space. In the spring His Majesty's ships would have appeared as usual, to the discomfort of Bermudians, but for a development in the field of diplomacy. The threat, converted by September into an actuality, of a French declaration of war on Great Britain, obliged the British admirals to abandon petty enterprises like the blockade of Bermuda and to concentrate in defense of the West Indies. From that time until 1781 no warship paid more than flying visits to Bermuda. In May the customs collector, Thomas Smith, pleaded in vain with Lord Howe for at least one vessel of the imperial navy. From that time he was compelled to do what he could with a tender and boat at the west end, which did little more than annoy the wily Bermudian mariners.[8]

Throughout 1776 and 1777 (winters apart) the blockade about the island had been more successful

---

[7] Henry Tucker, Sr., to St. George, January 13, April 2, June 22, 1777. T. H. P. Bruere to Germain, March 4 and April 19, 1777, cited above; complaint of council and assembly of Bermuda, July 8, 1779, in C.O. 37 vol. 22.

[8] Henry Tucker, Sr., to St. George, May 8, 1778, May 15, 1779. T. H. P.

than the dominant group of Bermudians had thought possible. In April 1777 Colonel Henry Tucker was confessing: "There is no coming here while these harpies are with us"; in July he mourned, "no vessels come near us as it is known everywhere what a lookout is kept for them"; and in October he repeated the tale of woe.[9] Nevertheless there was no immediate shortage of food for Captain Collins sold corn, rice and flour from his prizes at satisfactory rates to his own profit if islanders were correct in their suspicions. In the autumn supplies ran low even in Bruere's view, especially of Indian corn for the negroes.[10] But one day the tender left the west end for St. Georges and in her absence a small vessel with about one thousand bushels of corn slipped into a little inlet on the south side and discharged her cargo. As soon as the *Nautilus* had turned her back, sloops swarmed away from the island in search of provisions; and by December they had restocked it— "we are at present comfortably though not largely supplied."[11] The absence of the warships through 1778 permitted Bermudians and their American friends to bring in provisions as they would, save for the collector's feeble efforts, until the rise of another menace. By the end of 1778 the war had inflicted no serious hardship on Bermuda.

Indeed opportunities for a type of business congenial to the islanders were not lacking. A French brigantine, *L'Active*, was wrecked on the northwest rocks on December 30, 1777. The inhabitants of the locality saved the people on board and most of the

[9] Henry Tucker, Sr., to St. George, April 2, July 21, October 14, 1777. T. H. P.
[10] Bruere to Germain, October 14, 1777, in C. O. 37 vol. 36.
[11] Henry Tucker of Somerset to St. George, December 17, 1777. T. H. P.

cargo, refraining from plunder and thereby obtaining an honorable mention in Bruere's despatch. As reward for their efforts they received one-sixth of the cargo. But two other vessels were not so fortunate as *L'Active*. In February 1778 the ship *Lord Amherst*, Captain Hartwell, carrying invalid sailors, was wrecked off Bermuda. Some people of the west end assisted to save the invalids but only at a price; and when that price did not meet their expectations, they arrested Captain Hartwell. The governor and the customs collector were obliged to become securities to obtain the captain's release. Another difficulty arose about the cargo and rigging, much of which had been salved. Three local J. P.'s awarded the salvers a third of the gross sales of the indigo and rum, a half of all other goods. The owners, finding protests vain, secured George Bascome as their advocate and brought the matter before the council. That body held an enquiry and discovered that two of the J. P.'s concerned, Richard Fowler and Nathaniel Bell, had had boats engaged in the salvage. The governor therefore issued a new warrant for settlement of salvage by magistrates less directly interested.[12] The third vessel, a Spaniard commanded by Captain Xavier and carrying a certain Señor M. Framil as supercargo, was wrecked at the west end on March 31, 1778, and had the bad luck to fall into the hands of Henry Tucker of Somerset's gang. John, Dan and Robert Tucker went out to it in boats owned chiefly by their boss and the Jennings; and by some means they induced Captain Xavier to nominate them his agents to salve the 300,000 pounds of indigo on board. They removed it and took two-fifths for them-

[12] Bruere to Germain, March 24 and April 20, 1778, in C. O. 37 vol. 37; minutes of executive council, March 12, 1778. (Bermuda Archives.)

selves, allowing only their friends to share the work
and evoking an uproar of protest from other Bermudians while Colonel Henry Tucker, left out in the
cold, wrote enviously to St. George that the country
would be £30,000 or £40,000 richer by the affair.
Señor Framil, however, now intervened with a claim
that he alone was in charge of the cargo and that he
had not been consulted in the deal with the Tuckers.
Bruere heard the complaint and informed the Tuckers
that they could not be agents without his consent or
take the goods without first lodging them in the customs house; he then held a court and ordered the
Tuckers and Captain Xavier to deliver up their indigo.[13] Strange to say they did so, probably because
of the jealousy of other islanders; but they charged
very heavy salvage fees which no doubt came little
short of the two-fifths. It goes without saying that
Henry Tucker of Somerset was the chief gainer from
the business.

It will be seen that if one makes allowance for the
natural difficulties of war, Bermudians had little to
complain about until the autumn of 1778. But the
dominant families did not so view the matter. They
measured events solely by the economic standard,
found their opportunities for business limited by the
activities of His Majesty's ships, and conceived a
grievance. Hence they adopted a policy to which they
clung with a determination worthy of a better cause,
of harassing the governor and the navy. In July 1776
the council and assembly took the opportunity of a
session to despatch a long apology and complaint to
London. The preamble asseverated and particular-
ized Bermudian loyalty to His Majesty's person and

---

[13] Bruere to Germain, October 5, 1778, in C. O. 37 vol. 37; Henry Tucker,
Sr., to St. George, April 23 and May 8, 1778, in T. H. P.

family, the British constitution and government.
Therefore the petitioners had long regarded the unhappy differences between the mother country and
the American colonies with the utmost anxiety not
only as the source of misfortune to the empire "but
as the immediate fountain of a torrent of calamities
by which we are likely to be overwhelmed in this
unhappy island." First of these calamities had been
the American embargo. Hearing of this with terror,
they had applied to Congress in belief that a general
reconciliation was at hand, and had secured their
exemption. Next, Parliament's embargo fell on them
and "our souls thrilled with horror." They repudiated
complicity in the affair of the powder and alleged
their offer of a reward in proof of innocence. Having
finished their defense, they presented as prime grievance the action of the *Scorpion's* lieutenant in the
matter of the rice.

This version of events with its audacious falsifica-
tions can be regarded only as an attempt to bluff His
Majesty's government. Following Henry Tucker of
Somerset, the leaders of the assembly had fixed on
the policy of uttering loyal words as a smoke-screen
for obstructing the least action in favor of loyalty.
Their symbolic animal would have been the mule
who does not openly defy his master but will slyly
kick and bite. They sent the address to Lord George
Germain who, less intimately acquainted than Bruere
with local habits, was half inclined to believe the
protestations. He thought that the assembly's conduct appeared "far less culpable than I had reason
to believe from your account" though he acknowl-

edged "their actions leave room for great doubt and suspicion of their declarations."[14]

In the same session (July 1776) the assembly sought and found opportunities to annoy the governor. He asked them to repair the fortifications of the island. They replied with a touch of Henry Tucker of Somerset's humor that they could give no effective aid as the island was stripped of its powder and its cannon. Willing to waste time by an argument, they called the removal of the guns "an impolitic and unwarrantable proceeding" and asked whether it had been done by superior authority or the governor's own. He replied merely that he expected His Majesty's approbation. They sent another "long and aggravating" message complaining that they were being maligned to the King. They offered to exculpate themselves and the people from the least suspicion of having contributed to the theft of the powder, attributed the export of the cannon to "groundless whim or sinister motive" and assured Bruere of their readiness to watch every proceeding that might tend to the disadvantage of the public, to submit grievances to the King and to solicit the most ample justice to the inhabitants "of this most injured country." The pose of outraged innocence was no doubt calculated to delude simple loyalists and imperial authorities, who had just reconfirmed Bermudian privileges in the Turks Islands. It certainly did not delude Bruere, who dissolved the assembly by way of reply, useless as that constitutional exercise might seem to be.[15]

---

[14] Council and assembly to the King, July 12, 1776, in C. O. 37 vol. 36 and C. O. 40 vol. 20. Germain to Bruere, January 1, 1777, in C. O. 37 vol. 36.

[15] Bruere to Germain, July 14, 1776, in C. O. 37 vol. 36; minutes of assembly, June 28 to July 12, 1776, in C. O. 40 vol. 20.

In the ensuing interval of sessions, the council continued the policy of pinpricks by representing to the governor the "melancholy and truly calamitous situation" caused by a drought and especially by interruption of supplies from America. Bruere replied that he would do everything consistent with his duty to His Majesty and the supremacy of the British Empire, which limits were much too narrow for many islanders. In February 1777 the assembly bewailed the fatal consequences of the contest between mother country and colonies and hoped that His Majesty's subjects who had swerved from their allegiance might return to it. The affairs of Salt Kettle and the prisoner Wainwright now roused their indignation. Council and assembly appointed a committee which proceeded to take depositions on the conduct of Merrick and Jordan, and another to address Lord Howe. At this point Bruere prorogued them. Promptly five of the councillors (George Forbes, Jonathan Burch, John Harvey, Henry Tucker, Jr., John Hinson) incensed at the halting of their enquiry, sent the governor a letter expostulating on his action in face of the "repeated insults" and "violent outrages" committed by the sailors who had "entirely wrested the reins of administration" out of Bruere's hands and held the island's laws "in derision and contempt." The councillors concluded with a hint that if denied constitutional relief, the people might have recourse to physical resistance. But Bruere was not to be caught by the attempt to incite him against the captains in this "very provoking" letter. He replied with a stricture on the assembly's twenty-year-old habit of neglecting necessary business to take up matters that did not concern them and especially on their indifference to the £1000 arrears in his salary.[16] Meanwhile Lieutenant Merrick, asked to appear before the committee, had sent a reply from Ely's Harbor. "I beg, sir, that you will inform the committee that I am in no ways accountable to them for any part of my conduct as an officer in His Majesty's service. I shall treat their malicious efforts to injure me with every contempt in my power . . . a set of men devoid of principles or honor and who have on all occasions manifested themselves as rebels and enemies to their King and the mother country."[17]

Failing with Bruere and Merrick, the leaders of Bermuda had by no means come to the end of their resources. They arranged an informal election of delegates in the parishes who met at Crow Lane, drew up an address and appointed Henry Tucker, Jr., and Nathaniel Jones to take it to New York. These two proceeded to that city and sought an interview with the naval commanders. Lord Drummond received them courteously; Lord Howe heard their complaints and replied that he pitied their situation and would do all he could to help them short of countenancing their violation of an act of Parliament. He agreed that Captain Jordan had been acting unwisely and he indicated an intention of replacing him and his ship by Captain Chinnery and the *Daphne*. Finally he released Wainwright.[18] The delegation returned to Bermuda in high spirits, having obtained considerable

[16] Minutes of executive council, September 3, 1776, and April 22, 1777 (Bermuda Archives); minutes of assembly, February 13 to March 24, 1777, in C. O. 40 vol. 20; Bruere to Germain, March 24, 1777, in C. O. 37 vol. 36.

[17] Lieutenant W. A. Merrick to Mr. Lewis, clerk of the assembly, March 24, 1777, in C. O. 37 vol. 22. The assembly's comment on the reply was "He did by letter reflect on the committee in a very extraordinary and abusive manner." Complaint of July 8, 1779, in C. O. 37 vol. 22.

[18] Henry Tucker, Sr., to St. George, April 2 and June 22, 1777. T. H. P.

concessions. Shortly afterward Lord Howe reprimanded Jordan and removed him from the station;
but he did not send the *Daphne*, the *Nautilus* and her
auxiliaries sufficing.

Pleased at their success with Lord Howe, the members of council and assembly now thought to bear
their tale of wrong to the King. Balked by Bruere of
assuming their official capacities, they acted in their
private and in April composed an address to the sovereign. After the conventional protest that disaffec-
tion was abhorrent to them they complained of the
"pursuing with tenders and armed boats our little
vessels employed in the importation of provisions
to our doors and snatching from the very mouths of
our half-starved inhabitants the very means of subsistence." They recounted the deeds of the sailors and
concluded with another assertion of loyalty by way of
stage effect. This address they sent to a Mr. Taylor
in London, for presentation to Lord George Germain.
The secretary, however, was well informed by Bruere
and the Admiralty of islanders' delinquencies and
their liberal estimates of the danger of starvation.
John Robinson, secretary to the Lords of the Treasury, exclaimed "What, are those wretches in rebellion
too?" Germain pigeonholed the address and would
not receive Mr. Taylor.[19]

Foiled in London, the assembly could always return
to the pastime of bothering Bruere. In June 1777, on
the strength of a rumor that the Americans would
descend on Bermuda as they had done on the Bahamas the year before, the governor asked the lower
house what its members would do in case of invasion
and summoned them to take steps to meet it. They

[19] Members of council and assembly to the King, April 20, 1777, in C. O.
37 vol. 36. Henry Tucker, Sr., to St. George, October 14, 1777. T. H. P.

replied that they maintained a militia for such events, that they were willing to join the council to inspect the fortifications and that an invasion would find them ready to behave consistently "with the loyalty we have ever professed." Although the quality of that loyalty inspired little confidence, Bruere could secure no more than the profession. When they met again in July, the members piqued by the loss of several of their vessels and cargoes to the *Nautilus* and *Galatea*, seized the opportunity of their address to the governor to make reflections on the captains of their guardian ships. They then adopted bills to restrict export of provisions, fix their prices and limit the quantities vessels might take as stores. Bruere, enlightened by the incident of the *Scorpion*, requested exceptions for His Majesty's ships. The assembly, perhaps seeing the *raison d'être* of the bills at stake, refused; Bruere vetoed the bills and matters reverted to the status quo.[20] In the October session the assembly showed its temper by refusing money not only for fortifications but for the matrosses, the "four old men" who formed a skeleton staff in charge of the local fort at St. Georges. Bruere thereupon paid the matrosses out of his own pocket. The assembly next passed a set of resolutions in favor of free trade, i.e. with the Americans, which Bruere naturally found unacceptable. He answered shortly and adjourned them.[21] The absence of the warships in 1778 of course put the legislature in much better temper. On September 15 Bruere announced to the council that France had declared war and had disturbed some

[20] Minutes of assembly, June 28 to July 13, 1777, in C. O. 40 vol. 20; Williams, pp. 86-7. Bruere to Germain, July 14, 1777, in C. O. 37 vol. 36.
[21] Bruere to Germain, October 27 and November 1, 1777, in C. O. 37 vol. 36; minutes of assembly, October 10, 1777, in C. O. 40 vol. 20.

Bermudians at Turks Islands. He hoped that the insult would arouse the people of Bermuda to unite to defeat their enemies.[22] The exhortation was in vain; one may guess that the chief anxiety of the leading families at that moment was to contrive some accommodation with the new enemy which would save their trade.

In the meantime an incident had happened which illustrated Bermudian sentiments from another angle. In June 1777 an American privateer arrived under a Bermudian, Frank Morgan. Showing British colors, he came to Hogfish Cut and intended to put in; but the garrison there suspected him and fired at him. He returned a broadside which fell much short, then stood out to sea and hoisted the Stars and Stripes. Presently a second privateer appeared under another Morgan. The officer in charge of the fort became alarmed and abandoned it that evening, taking off the utensils and powder. The tender and boat, also alarmed, went off to St. Georges. The coast being now clear, the second brig came in next morning and anchored in the snapper ground. Its crew landed, spiked the guns, broke the carriages and destroyed part of the breast-work. At night they sent a party into Somerset and took some eight-carriage guns, the property of Mrs. Seymour. They then lay six days at the cut and finally went out at their leisure. All this while the *Nautilus* lay snug in Castle Harbor twenty miles away, though much stronger than both privateers together. Captain Collins alleged as excuse for inaction a report that the brig was a decoy to bring him within range of a large American vessel, the *Randolph*; and took care to put his money on shore. Thereby he earned sharp criticism from the

[22] Minutes of executive council, September 15, 1778. (Bermuda Archives.)

islanders who alleged that "gain and not any regard to the service is his chief inducement." Eventually he fitted out a captured sloop with guns and in company with her made his appearance on the north side just when the brig had left the cut. He then stationed the sloop in Ely's Harbour, lay for a while himself in the sound near the Bridge, and shortly sent a detachment which restored the fort. Throughout the business the local Bermudians took the visit of the privateers very ill, fearing it might exasperate the government against them and bring a sloop of war to do constant duty at the west end. In Colonel Henry Tucker's opinion they would even have turned out in arms against the Morgans and Americans had Bruere summoned them.[23] For where local interests were concerned, they were sensitive to the quick, against Americans as all others.

[23] Henry Tucker, Sr., to St. George, June 22 and 29, 1777. T. H. P.

CHAPTER V

BERMUDA AND THE PRIVATEERS

THE rejoicings of the islanders in 1778 over their liberation from His Majesty's vigilant ships were shortly curtailed. For the removal of the ships brought up the question of a garrison. Lord George Germain, pressed by Bruere, had meditated sending troops to Bermuda as early as January 1, 1777; but on news of a revolt among the slaves in Jamaica, he diverted the force to that colony. The prayers of Bruere moved him only to condemn "the very disorderly and undutiful behavior of the assembly and inhabitants of Bermuda." In 1778 he finally secured a detachment for the islands, two companies commanded by Major William Sutherland which arrived on November 2. These were reinforced on December 1, 1779, by a party of one hundred men under Lieutenant-Colonel Donkin who had narrowly escaped being cut off by four American frigates.[1] From this time Bermuda had a garrison and Bruere felt some security.

Having no enemy in arms to meet, the troops made it their business to aid the collector in suppressing contraband trade. For this purpose the commander sent a party to the west end who speedily fell foul of the inhabitants. The soldiers captured one vessel, set it on fire and stood around with bayonets to prevent the neighbors from extinguishing the flames while the owner and his friends appealed in vain to the commanding officer. An alarm having been raised

[1] Germain to Bruere, January 7, 1778; Bruere to Germain, November 6, 1778, and December 2, 1779. C. O. 37 vol. 37.

that Colonel Henry Tucker was moving Boston to send an expedition to the islands, the commanding officer erected a fort on private property without the owner's consent. Major Sutherland seized for himself a house occupied by Copeland Stiles but owned by Edward Stiles, now residing in Philadelphia and a sympathizer with the Americans; he cut short objections by turning the family out. The soldiers received an allowance from the assembly of £300 currency for firewood, but found it not enough and helped themselves freely to whatever timber was available, taking some that had been collected for a house, and stripping Councillor Henry Tucker's land of trees worth £50 sterling. In their zeal for their work the military even overstepped the bounds of legality. Some soldiers went aboard suspect vessels without the supervision of customs officers; but Bruere put a stop to this practice. Others seized a vessel after she had been cleared and unloaded; still others took in charge a condemned sloop, the *Southampton*, and put sentries on her, apparently against the wish of the customs officers. Reports of these doings soon reached New York; and General Sir H. Clinton reprimanded the officer responsible for the *Southampton* affair, rebuked Sutherland and removed him from command of the garrison battalion.[2] But the operations against contraband continued and with considerable success though perhaps not with the complete effectiveness of the *Nautilus* and *Galatea*. His Majesty's ships, looking in at Bermuda from time to time lent some aid: Captain Collins of the *Camilla* seized a brigantine belonging to Forbes and took it to New York in spite of its admission to customs.

[2] Articles of complaint by council and assembly, July 8, 1779; Bruere to Germain, March 25 and April 5, 1780, in C. O. 37 vol. 22.

The troops, however, received aid from another source. The Bermudians had an ideal base from which to operate as privateers against His Majesty's rebel subjects, as they had done against French and Spanish in the Seven Years War. They could have fitted out sixty or seventy swift vessels with the utmost ease to prey on American commerce. Yet, strange as it seemed to observers, Bermudians lifted no hand against American ships; and when the French entered the war, they extended to them a like courtesy. But the opportunity for a lucrative business ignored by islanders became apparent to outsiders. In the winter of 1777-1778, Captain Neale, a nephew of Mrs. Bruere and also a son-in-law when he married Harriet Bruere in the next year, began to engage in privateering. But he declared that he had no intention of disturbing any native, and on this evidence of good nature was tolerated. Another was not so scrupulous. Bridger Goodrich, a refugee from Virginia, settled in St. Georges in that winter and fitted out a privateer. By the end of January 1778 he had taken nine prizes, seven Americans and two Bermudians laden with Indian corn, thus showing unusual enterprise.[3] For a time thereafter he abstained from troubling native sloops; and as long as he confined his attention to American vessels, most Bermudians looked on his business with great equanimity. But the Tuckers and their friends sensed uneasily the rise of the cloud no bigger than a man's hand; they forbore to do business with the privateers or have any communication with them, leaving that traffic to persons "mercenary" or "inattentive to the consequences." In the summer Goodrich changed his

[3] Bruere to Germain, January 25, 1778, in C. O. 37 vol. 37.

policy again and announced that he would take any Bermudian loaded with anything but provisions; and in August he carried the threat into action, took a local vessel and sent her to New York. Thus he attacked the most sensitive spot, local interests. Indignation was general and when he returned at the beginning of September, some spoke of destroying his privateer and him. But the vigilant dominant families saw an opportunity of converting the wrath at one man into a general rising against privateering. They held a public meeting at Crow Lane and advocated a boycott of Goodrich and his like. Those present entered into a "general association" to hold no commercial or other intercourse with privateers and resolved to enter suit against Goodrich for the vessel he had taken to New York in order either to drive him from the island or harass him if he remained. Any transgressor of the rules would be reported to the continent and his business with it thereby terminated.[4] Henry Tucker of Somerset, John Harvey and George Bascome were the moving spirits of this association, the last becoming its clerk or secretary; and enough assemblymen joined them to make a proportion of fully three-fourths of their house. Thus the association was applying to Goodrich the very principle so distasteful when forced on them by the British government, that of no truck or trade with the enemy. They next took legal ground, claimed that Bermudian vessels were exempt from seizure by any but His Majesty's ships and brought suit against the privateers. The contention of course could not stand in court against official letters of marque. But George

---

[4] Henry Tucker, Sr., to St. George, April 23 and September 4, 1778; Henry Tucker of Somerset to St. George, September 10, 1778, in T. H. P. William Brimage to Germain, undated 1780, in C. O. 37 vol. 37.

Bascome brought suit on obscure grounds against a loyalist named William Honey and aided by the delays of Chief Justice Burch in dealing with the case, prevented the man from going on a privateering expedition.[5] So speedily had the privateers instructed the leading Bermudians in the value of the British law which they had long held in little esteem. The assembly now took part in the campaign and by a revenue bill of January 1779 placed taxes on rum, slaves, horses, tonnage, cedar timber and on prizes of privateers at 3¾%, the last item probably forming the *raison d'être* of the measure. The bill preluded by a provision for the troops came to Bruere as he lay ill and he signed it without knowing what he was doing. The owners of privateers promptly protested; and Bruere in agony that he had been deluded, prayed the home authorities to disallow the act.[6] Nevertheless it remained on the statute books for more than a year. The west enders, directed by Henry Tucker of Somerset, aided the association to the best of their ability. Captain Pendor of the British privateer *Triumph* several times called at the west end under British colors and could not procure even one small boat in answer to his call for information and supplies. In 1780 he changed his tactics and by advice of his lieutenant, a Bermudian, he hoisted the Stars and Stripes. At once fourteen or fifteen boats swarmed out and offered every kind of assistance. Meanwhile members of the association carried out their agreement not to sell to the privateers or treat them as other than outcasts; and once at least they made use of force.[7]

[5] Charges of George Bruere against the council of Bermuda, 1782, in C. O. 37 vol. 38.
[6] Bruere to Germain, October 4, 1779, in C. O. 37 vol. 37.
[7] George Bruere to Germain, January 7, 1781, in C. O. 37 vol. 38.

But Goodrich had even less mind than his antagonists to sit quietly under an embargo imposed by other people. He first essayed a breach in the social boycott against him. He made addresses to Elizabeth Tucker, niece of the colonel; and the lady, with a better eye for a man than her uncle, married him much to that uncle's disgust. Resuming business, he did not careen in St. Georges in September as he had intended but under the very nose of the association he secured supplies for another voyage. Though with difficulty, he always found some Bermudian to sell him what he wanted, and he never lacked supplies. He was even able to buy a boat of sorts from Godet though no one else would accept his offers. The lawsuits he defeated without trouble. Even the tax on privateers failed to halt his progress; at the end of February 1779 Colonel Henry Tucker admitted with a tinge of jealousy that Goodrich was making money. The other privateers had been frightened to some extent at the formation of the association; but on the arrival of the troops in November 1778 they took heart and resumed operations, capturing a French ship from Nantes and two or three small American vessels. Some Scots merchants arrived from New York to share in the occupation; and by February they, Neale and Goodrich, had all the active business in Bermuda. Finding difficulty in securing supplies on the island, they stocked up easily enough in New York. By 1780 ninety-one prizes had passed through admiralty court and the port of St. Georges had become "a considerable rendezvous and mart." Bridger Goodrich had defeated the boycott; he had paid the leading Bermudians in their own coin and they did not like it.[8]

From this flourishing business two important consequences flowed. The first affected stocks of food in the island. The privateers and the troops harried the traders in contraband and remaining the year around, unlike the *Nautilus* and the *Galatea*, reduced them to straits. As early as February 1779, Governor Bruere realized that supplies were becoming dangerously low. For the first time he departed from his policy of strict obedience to the prohibitions of Parliament, and issued a limited number of licenses for trade with the states in revolt. In April an American ship arrived with provisions and he permitted her cargo to be landed and distributed among the people. Soon another American ship arrived from Charleston under Captain Nathaniel King with a similar cargo but would not venture in without assurances of immunity from seizure. The governor gave these; but Collector Thomas Smith, fearing loss of his fees, swore he would seize the sloop and secured the support of the military.[9] In these circumstances the cargo went elsewhere and another sloop from Charleston also shied away while Bermudians suffered for lack of food. "We have been in a most deplorable situation," reported Bruere in May, "not a tenth part sufficient hath arrived for our numerous inhabitants."[10] He continued the policy of licenses, Colonel Henry Tucker eagerly seizing the opportunity to convert illicit into legal business, but found

[8] Henry Tucker, Sr., to St. George, February 24, 1779, in T. H. P.; William Brimage to Germain, undated 1780, in C. O. 37 vol. 37.

[9] Henry Tucker, Sr., to St. George, February 24, and May 15, 1779. T. H. P.

[10] Bruere to Germain, May 1, 1779, in C. O. 37 vol. 37.

that it barely met the need. The islanders might have had recourse to cultivating their soil for supplies, as did several West Indian colonies: but such an expedient they refused to consider even in extremity.

The second consequence of the privateering was that feared by the leaders of the association. News of the capture of American vessels by privateers from Bermuda rapidly spread to the continent. Congress could not but consider these as hostile acts; and in the autumn of 1778 in issuing new regulations about the export of provisions, it omitted the list of excepted colonies in which Bermuda had held first place. Island mariners were resourceful enough to find many Americans willing to sell provisions in great indifference to the orders of Congress; but they would now be obliged to run the gauntlet of American privateers as well as those of British navy and British privateers. They promptly appealed to Congress for modifications of the orders. John Lightbourn, having learned of the new regulations while in Philadelphia with a cargo of salt and West Indian produce, petitioned for revocation on November 12, 1778, pleading that the islanders were in a "starving and distressed situation." Congress, perhaps acquainted with an exaggeration in petitioners' requests, rejected the prayer. Next, twenty of the most prominent leaders of Bermuda, Tuckers, Jennings, Bascomes and others, sent a restrained memorial to Philadelphia in March 1779, recalling previous privileges and pleading for their continuance.[11] Three mariners, Leonard Albouy, Joseph Basden, Nathaniel Prudden, armed with a license from Bruere, appeared in Philadelphia in

[11] Papers of Continental Congress, no. 42, VI, folio 423; no. 41, I, folios 176-7.

April and after the first had applied to Jay for an export permit, also tried their hands at a petition for changed regulations. By way of stage effect they described British armed forces as "the common enemy" and depicted Bermudians as to the extent of nine-tenths desirous of joining in the American revolt and held back only by the prospect of certain destruction by the British navy. In a second communication, Albouy, Basden and W. Murray elaborated on the anti-privateering association and the tax on prizes as reasons for favor to Bermuda.[12]

Congress was divided in mind about the request. A committee composed of Ellery, Fell and Laurens recommended charity to the islanders; and finding some opposition from Burke and Morris, made a serious effort on May 18, declaring their conviction that the distress was not exaggerated. They stated that they had collected a number of important vouchers in proof of the warm attachment of Bermudians to the States and had secured French sanction for any necessary relief. Congress therefore allowed export of a thousand bushels of corn from each of five States.[13] For some time Congress adhered to this policy of maintaining the prohibition of export but granting permits to certain Bermudians to violate it from time to time. In August 1780 the same Joseph Basden petitioned for intervention on his behalf with the French who had seized his sloop at Turks Islands; and a committee supported the request on the ground that the inhabitants of Bermuda in general "appear to maintain the good disposition toward these United States which induced

[12] Papers of Continental Congress, no. 41, I, folio 35; no. 78, I, folios 241, 253, 267.
[13] Journals of Continental Congress, XIII, 471; XIV, 501, 555, 595, 608.

Congress . . . to consider them in a friendly or at least in a neutral relation" and had acted equally as neutrals toward the French. When in the same month William Murray, master of the *Betsey and Nancy* of Bermuda, asked permission to change his salt for American flour and corn, Congress gladly accorded it to him.[14] But the activities of the privateers from Bermuda, increasing by leaps and bounds, finally brought about a change in this policy. In March 1781 Congress resolved to repeal all exceptions in favor of Bermuda, the order to come into effect on May 1. The delegates of Virginia secured an exception for themselves, a permission to import 50,000 bushels of Bermudian salt; in September a committee tried to broaden this concession into a general free trade in that commodity, in vain; and thereafter official commercial relations came to an end.[15] Bridger Goodrich and his friends had finally succeeded in breaking the alliance between the leaders of Bermuda and the Continental Congress. Unofficially of course trade relations continued between Bermudian mariners and their American friends, though subject to hazards from armed vessels of all sorts.

Long before this rupture the Bermudians had suffered severely from the cumulation of interruptions to their food supply. Importations by the governor's license and sales of captured cargoes by privateers afforded several "providential but temporary" reliefs in the summer of 1779, but as autumn came on, failed to meet the demand. "We are all in a melancholy situation here at present," wrote Mrs. Henry Tucker

[14] Journals of the Continental Congress, XVII, 694, 795.
[15] Letters of Members of the Continental Congress, VI, 37, 170, 180, 191, edited by E. C. Burnett, Washington, Carnegie Institute, 1933; Journals, XXI, 959-60.

of Somerset; "numbers of people have died for want or for feeding on such food as has brought disorders that has [*sic*] killed them." Her sister Eliza Tucker echoed the opinion in November 1779. "Our unhappy country feels the severest of ills . . . thousands have suffered and many have perished for want of bread." Corn and peas brought in a prize had been sold at public auction for more than 20s. a bushel; fresh meats and poultry had become a rarity, butter and eggs scarce and dear. "Our living is indeed most wretched." Eliza of course had her own analysis of the responsibility. "Such are the good effects of our being overrun with soldiers and privateers and of the ill conduct of a misjudging governor."[16]

The scarcity of food was not the only problem on the island at the time. In the previous winter the prisoners, chiefly American, in the congested jails had fallen victims to a sickness which had spread to the islanders. "I never knew it so sickly here," wrote Henry Tucker, Jr., in the spring of 1779, "as it has been this whole winter . . . nothing but wretchedness in extreme offers itself to my view." All summer the malady persisted; and a year later a friend of his wrote to the same effect: "Very few families have escaped from a prevailing disorder called the camp fever."[17] Many deaths occurred and difficulties in Bermuda reached a maximum. In the spring and summer of 1780, however, Bermudian ingenuity discovered ways to evade the privateers and replenish the stocks of food; and the worst experiences of the war came to an end.

[16] Mrs. Henry Tucker of Somerset to St. George Tucker, November 26, 1779; Eliza Tucker to St. George, November 25, 1779.
[17] Henry Tucker, Jr., to St. George, April 18, 1779; John Darrell to St. George, May 1780. All in T. H. P.

At the first signal of approaching troubles in 1779 the assembly had resumed its policy of obstructing governor and troops. On January 15 they protested to Bruere about the conduct of the soldiers at the west end who were preventing the importation of provisions and asked for their removal. Next day the council seconded the motion by complaints that the troops had misbehaved and "in many respects injured the inhabitants." Bruere replied sharply that he had sent the soldiers there to perform a necessary duty and that the assembly ought to set the people a good example by refraining from words to the prejudice of government. Some months later he lectured them on the evil of slavery which was responsible for such indolence in the poor whites that they would do nothing to help themselves, presumably by tilling the soil. The assembly in reply did not discuss this sore point but reiterated their loyalty which quite justified their actions since "these sentiments impel us to oppose every wanton exercise of power." This peculiarly negative conception of loyalty may be due to Henry Tucker of Somerset's reading of Junius. In conclusion they requested the governor to appoint more justices of the peace, in the interest of legal impediments to the actions of soldiers and privateers; but Bruere was not to be hoodwinked thus.[18]

Failing to make headway against troops, privateers and governor, the leading families struck on the idea of sending a special agent to London who might get the ear of the Colonial Secretary and embarrass all three. With supreme assurance they selected Colonel Henry Tucker who had done them such good service in Philadelphia. The council felt some compunction

[18] Assembly minutes, January 15-17, May 12-14, 1779, in C. O. 40 vol. 20; minutes of executive council, January 16, 1779. (Bermuda Archives.)

about the choice, only Henry Tucker, Jr., and Chief Justice Burch acceding with their signatures, but chosen he was. Next came the question of salary and expenses. Assembly and council passed a bill to raise £2000 to cover these; but Bruere, seeing necessary services and his own salary neglected, vetoed it. A joint committee of both houses then determined to raise a sum by subscription and to prepare an address to the King. Bruere promptly interfered with a prorogation. The members of the committee, not to be baffled, met by themselves and agreed to execute the plan in their private capacities, relying on a future session of the legislature for repayment. They had not long to wait; in July the assembly reduced the allowance to £500 a year, which Bruere accepted. They appointed a committee for correspondence with him, Henry Tucker of Somerset, John Jennings, Sam Harvey, George Bascome, James Tucker, the five of whom and especially the first had throughout guided the assembly's policy. Old Henry Tucker accepted the arrangement and went off in July, "very hearty and cheerful in hopes of doing good for his country," as his daughter wrote. He arrived in London early in August and was "well received." He set himself to remove the "strong prejudice" caused by the governor's representations but found that the Colonial Office, though suffering him through ignorance of his misdeeds, paid scant attention to him. A change took place nevertheless but the change was in Henry Tucker. Gradually he came to love London and to understand in part the imperial point of view and from that time he exercised a moderating influence on his friends in Bermuda,[19] urging them to abandon

[19] Henry Tucker, Sr., to St. George, June 3, and December 27, 1779; Bruere to Germain, June 1, and July 14, 1779, in C. O. 37 vol. 37. Mrs.

even the anti-privateering association and to live on terms with the home authorities.

Bruere had dissolved the assembly again in July, to the usual little purpose. The nominally new legislature met in October (1779) and addressed him on their favorite remedy for the scarcity, the opening of the ports of the island to all who should bring provisions. Bruere replied that he could not trust the avaricious temper of the people to that extent but was willing to license one vessel from each parish to trade anywhere for provisions, i.e., to the States in arms. In the course of several exchanges they protested plaintively that his general censure was undeserved, his remedy insufficient, his making light of their poverty a heartless procedure. They mourned "the unfeeling obduracy of heart which seems to breathe through the whole of your address" and their own fate in having a governor "who appears rather disposed to trifle with our distress, to insult our misfortunes than to promote any probable method of relieving them." At their own request he then adjourned them until November. When they had met in the middle of that month, a committee reported on the condition of the jails. They had found a nauseous stench and in it twenty Americans, some sick, who received raw rice once a day and else subsisted on charity. The assembly made this a matter of complaint to the governor. He, producing a circular of instructions from Whitehall, replied that it was their duty to vote funds for the care of the prisoners. They passed the responsibility back to the British government, protesting their loyalty for lack of an argument. They had been ready to find £2000

Henry Tucker of Somerset to St. George, November 26, 1779, in T. H. P. Kaye, p. 4, for Colonel Henry's love of London.

for Henry Tucker, Sr., but could not discover a penny for the sick and starving prisoners, thereby revealing the extent of their interest in Americans out of whom no money was to be made. Humbler Bermudians proved more merciful by assisting the prisoners to escape. The assembly now appointed a committee which with some councillors investigated the condition of the forts, found it bad and could not imagine what was to be done, unless the British government should spend some money on them. Of course the real motive throughout was to use the governor as a whipping-boy for the troops and privateers.[20]

In April 1780 Bruere tried persuasion on them, hoping "to find you all disposed to support regular government and to manifest your loyalty to your King and your affection to your Mother Country from whence your forefathers sprung and not from America, France or Spain." Finding the appeal vain, in May he lectured them again on their repeated attempts to deviate from the mode and constitution of Great Britain as illustrated in their inclination toward paper money and the tax on privateers' prizes, and assured them in hot tones that he would consent to no more such vagaries. By reply they endeavored to repeal the act about his salary in order to substitute currency certificates for sterling as method of payment and thereby lessen the value by a third, which Bruere naturally refused. Finally the House resolved to petition His Majesty about the misery arising from the governor's administration and sent two members to request an adjournment. He well aware of the intention, turned his back on them, declared that their house was already adjourned and

[20] Minutes of assembly, October 11-16, 1779, in C. O. 40 vol. 17; of same dates and November 16-20, in C. O. 37 vol. 37.

that he would have no communication with them.[21] That was the last of his bickerings with the legislature of Bermuda; for in July and August he lay painfully ill and on September 10 he expired.

But the struggle between privateers and Bermudians had not yet fulfilled its consequences. The news about the anti-privateering association and the tax on prizes, late and shamefacedly revealed by Bruere, had led the home authorities to intervene once more. They decided to strengthen the government of Bermuda with fresh and vigorous blood; and in mid-1780 they appointed Bruere's son George as lieutenant-governor, Daniel Leonard of Barbados as attorney-general, Andrew Cazneau as judge of vice-admiralty and Robert Traill as customs collector. The last was a Scotsman formerly in office at Piscataqua; he now had orders to displace Collector Thomas Smith in Bermuda and recover a considerable sum of money in possession of that official. All of these men except Leonard set sail immediately, and reached the island in October and November. There was to be a serious attempt to reduce the Bermudians to order.[23]

[21] Minutes of assembly, April 10 to May 27, 1780, in C. O. 40 vol. 20, and Bruere to Germain, May 29, 1780, in C. O. 37 vol. 37. Williams, pp. 86-7.

[22] Germain to Bruere, July 5 and 7, 1780, in C. O. 37 vol. 37.

[23] A sketch of Leonard's life appears in the *Dictionary of American Biography*, XI, 174-5.

CHAPTER VI

LIEUTENANT-GOVERNOR GEORGE BRUERE

AT the death of Bruere, Thomas Jones, president of the council, took over the administration until the lieutenant-governor could arrive. His tenure was the opportunity for which the dominant families had been long in wait. He met the council on September 21 and proceeded to install the leaders of opposition in places of power. They chose officers of militia; Thomas Jones himself colonel, Henry Tucker of Somerset lieutenant-colonel, John Noble Taylor major, Thomas and Dan Tucker captain and lieutenant respectively of Sandys parish, Benjamin and Nathaniel Bascome captain and lieutenant of Warwick. Two days later the council recommended Henry Tucker and Joseph Jauncey as J. P.'s, of Sandys parish.[1] The assembly met about the same time. Henry Tucker of Somerset moved condolence to Mrs. Bruere but overlooked the arrears of her husband's salary; the assembly congratulated Thomas Jones on taking charge of the government, "a native from whom we have every reason to expect the most perfect attachment to His Majesty and attention to the welfare of these islands." The interpretation of the welfare was made clear by a motion from Henry Tucker of Somerset on September 23, complaining of Bruere's order to all vessels to come to St. Georges for customs inspection as a measure productive of great expense and risk to the people. That day the assembly passed a bill to use the proceeds of the liquor tax for

[1] Minutes of executive council, September 21 and 23, 1780. (Bermuda Archives.)

the salary of Colonel Henry Tucker in London and another revenue act renewing the tax on privateers' prizes. Thomas Jones assented to these. Thus the leading clique had well entrenched themselves and established their policy before the new officers of government could arrive.[2]

George Bruere, eldest son of his father, had early chosen the army as his profession and had served with the 14th Foot in the Seven Years War. Retired on half pay from 1763, he had resumed service with the 18th Foot as lieutenant in 1769 and had been in garrison at Philadelphia in 1772. In 1775 he was with Gage's army in Boston and was wounded at Bunker Hill. Sent as invalid to Britain, he had plied Lord George Germain with accounts of the unpatriotic activities of the islanders. For a period in 1776-1777 he was in St. Augustine as captain of the 60th Foot; but thereafter he had been recalled in order to receive his new commission.[3] Rumors of the appointment had early reached Colonel Henry Tucker in London who had warned the secretary against "the warm temper and prejudices" of the lieutenant-governor and, failing, had gloomily surmised the advent of a scourge for Bermuda.[4] On the island, John Esten, a friend of the Tuckers, was preparing himself for the worst. "Our trade, I suppose, will be much cramped, but after all the industrious will live."[5]

Young, full of courage and energy, burning with

[2] Minutes of assembly, September 23, 1780, in C. O. 37 vol. 37.

[3] George Bruere's military career in a communication to the author by the editor of the *Journal of the Society for Army Historical Research*, March 15, 1935; also in Governor Bruere to St. George Tucker, December 15, 1772 and Henry Tucker, Sr., to St. George, November 5, 1777, in T. H. P.

[4] Henry Tucker, Sr., to Henry Tucker of Somerset, August 8, 1780, in C. O. 37 vol. 38.

[5] To St. George Tucker, October 9, 1780. T. H. P.

loyalty to the Empire, George Bruere set about the task of cleaning the Augean stables of his father's islands. He took the oath on October 5 and gave out that he would forget the past if the sinners would offend no more. He made a concession in respect of customs clearances at St. Georges in the hope of stimulating goodwill. Then he selected two points for immediate attack: the need of the troops, still suffering from camp fever, for a hospital, and the repeal of the revenue law of September 23. Proceeding circumspectly at first, on October 10 he informed the assembly that this law was contrary to royal instructions and acts of Parliament. The assembly asked to see the instructions; and he communicated a letter of Germain's in condemnation of the tax on prizes and a written opinion to the same effect by His Majesty's Advocate-General William Wynne, at the same time requesting assistance for the sick soldiers. Joint committees of council and assembly thereupon considered the documents and soon declared a belief that their law was not repugnant to acts of Parliament and its circumstances not fully known to Lord George Germain. But the members of the council, now including Traill, felt the need of a concession; and their committee, John Harvey dissenting, advised suspension of the law until His Majesty's pleasure could be known. The committee of assembly, led by Henry Tucker of Somerset, refused the advice and persuaded the house to reject suspension on the ostensible ground of financial need. Perhaps thinking to temper the effects of this action, they resolved to build a hospital for the troops. But George Bruere would not be put off so, and promptly dissolved them.[6]

    [6] George Bruere to Germain, December 12, 1780, in C. O. 37 vol. 38; minutes of assembly, October 9-13, 1780, in C. O. 40 vol. 18.

A short experience had shown him the lukewarmness of certain members of council. Relying on the support of Traill he suspended three members, John Hinson on ground of insanity, Thomas Jones for signing the bill of September 23 without reference to higher authority and John Harvey as a disaffected person, concerned in trade with rebels. That he stayed his hand at these three was due to the advice of Traill. The election of course made little difference to the composition of the assembly. He met it on November 23 and delivered a carefully thought speech. He declared that he would not execute the law of September and he pressed for its repeal. He urged the members to meet more regularly; he requested the hospital, repairs to the forts and provision for some sort of police and for his own salary. He desired permission for the soldiers to supplement their rations by fishing. He then broached the topic he had most at heart and summoned the legislature to break all confederations and associations tending to help rebels or enemies and not to follow any set of men led by sordid views of gain.

The members could not but pay some heed to the pressure, although they may have paid more to the admonitions of Colonel Henry in London that they should at least make a show of living on terms with the ministry. They knew also of the successes of British arms in Georgia and the Carolinas and judged it politic to curry a little favor with the side which might after all prove victorious. Accordingly the two houses appointed committees, Henry Tucker, Sam Trott, Robert Traill for the council, Henry Tucker of Somerset, Copeland Stiles, Henry Trott, George Bascome, John Jennings for the house. These men conferred on November 25, maintained their defense

of the tax on prizes as a financial measure only but
yielded the main point in recommending suspension
until His Majesty's pleasure be known "in order to
evince at the present period to His Majesty and the
world the clearest disinclination in the public of
Bermuda to move in opposition to what may be conceived by administration necessary to the service of
His Majesty." The assembly complied with the advice, suspended its rules and rushed through a bill to
that effect and another about the hospital; then
addressed the lieutenant-governor on what they had
done.[7] George Bruere had gained both of his points.

He now bent himself to the task of bringing order
into the administration of Bermuda. The first body
in need of attention was the council. Its members
were unreliable because the expense and trouble of
serving had kept out the suitable men on the island.
The unsuitable, who had accepted seats, had joined
in cabal with the leaders of the assembly to draw
most of the power into their hands and had thereby
reduced the governor to a cipher. The first duty of
the reformer in these circumstances was to eject the
unworthy and substitute better if such could be
found. George Bruere had already made a beginning
by the suspensions of October and the admission of
Robert Traill. He appointed Cazneau on the latter's
arrival in November and Major William Anstruther
in March (1781), both of whom rendered him most
loyal help. He desired to appoint others but could
come upon none of the proper qualifications; and
from time to time he meditated more suspensions but
refrained at the instance of his own supporters who
thought it unwise to cast all the natives forth from

[7] Assembly minutes of November 23-25, 1780, in C. O. 40 vol. 18; George
Bruere to Germain, December 12, 1780, in C. O. 37 vol. 38.

the council. Nevertheless he now had a council with which he could usually work. Meanwhile he had devoted attention to the demerits of the officers of government. Collector Thomas Smith had left his accounts in a sad state of confusion; but Traill was making some headway with them. Randle the late judge of admiralty had left many things "strangely undecided" and his office and papers "in a most bewildered situation." Here Cazneau fell to work and presently began to see glimmerings of light. But Randle had also been deputy secretary and provost marshal. He had never received any assistance from the assembly toward the maintenance of a safe house for the deeds; he had rented a building at his own expense and a fire had wrought havoc with the documents. Now he fell ill while his affairs as secretary lapsed into chaos and quitrents from crown lands went uncollected.[8] The lieutenant-governor dunned him for the accounts of powder moneys and quitrents; and in the absence of a reply proposed to the council to suspend him (June 1781). The council advised a final warning; and on its failure, suggested a post-ultimate application to the delinquent.[9] Randle's death (September or October 1781), however, closed the personal phase of the controversy. Next came the turn of Chief Justice Jonathan Burch. He had engaged in a personal quarrel with Captain Jordan and from that time had discovered all manner of legal obstacles to the most necessary operations of government. In the case of George Bascome versus William Honey, he had allowed delays which had, as we have seen, prevented Honey from privateering. Further Burch had been

[8] George Bruere to Germain, January 7, 1781, in C. O. 37 vol. 38; March 26, 1781, in same.

[9] Minutes of executive council, June 20 and 24, 1781 (Bermuda Archives).

corresponding from the council board itself with Bascome, "the rebel lawyer," to disclose to the lower house whatever secrets the upper had, presumably in particular the governor's opinions and policies. In March 1781 therefore Bruere suspended the chief justice and replaced him pro tempore by the loyalist refugee William Brimage. The latter had been acting as attorney-general; he now yielded the post to a certain Graham, a refugee from Virginia who held it until the arrival of Palmer, the substitute for Leonard. The lieutenant-governor thus secured a staff on which he could rely. The militia officers appointed by Jones in September, including Jones himself and Henry Tucker of Somerset, received short shrift; Bruere proclaimed their commissions null and void and warned the rank and file not to obey them. All the officers of government were now brought to heel. But Bruere saw that by these changes he could not effect a cure of the administrative maladies of Bermuda; he therefore advised the appointment of an able chief justice from home, independent of local connections, and the allotment of secure salaries to the principal officials who had hitherto depended on fees.[10]

With administration, finance went hand in hand. The new appointments and the new competence soon brought the treasury into "a better way than it has long been." By March there was actually a surplus of £2500 currency, the like of which had not been seen before. Bruere now took in hand the matter of fees on whales, which had been insidiously kept from his father to the amount of £1500 through the artifices of Burch and the whale company. He an-

[10] George Bruere to Germain, March 26, 1781, cited above.

nounced that he would seize every whale not paid on; and by his orders Lieutenant David Davis at the west end did seize one, thereby subduing the whalers. So far the lieutenant-governor had accomplished much; but to his own mind he had made only a beginning. The islands would require the united efforts of many to reduce them to good government. Nor were the generality of inhabitants blameless; they ought to cultivate the soil but would not do so, alleging apprehension of plunder by slaves. Most was yet wrong and little right in the economy and politics of Bermuda.[11]

The defects of administration and finance, however, were trifles compared to the prime offense of the islanders. Before he arrived, George Bruere had had some acquaintance with the trade carried on to and from the states in revolt; but he soon found his expectations far surpassed. For ingenious Bermudians had discovered in late years a number of ways in which they could carry on business in spite of the privateers. They built or secured ships which could leave the island in perfect legality and become merchantable commodities in neutral ports. In 1780 there were said to be one hundred vessels on the stocks in Bermuda intended for sale to the Americans by this method[12]; and Bruere calculated that since 1775 over one thousand craft had reached the same purchasers by way of St. Eustatia, most built in the islands, the rest fast-sailing prizes bought and refitted for the traffic. The Bermudians were in fact the mainstay of American privateering. The use of St. Eustatia

[11] George Bruere to Germain, March 26, 1781, cited above; December 12, 1780, cited above; complaint of council and assembly to Crown, July 29, 1782, in C.O. 37 vol. 38. The whalers took their case to court and lost.

[12] William Brimage to Germain, undated 1780, in C.O. 37 vol. 37.

came to a stop when Holland entered the war in
1780; but enterprising islanders soon found an effective substitute in the Danish possessions of St.
Thomas and St. Croix. Thus had sprung up a lively
business in export. But certain masters of sloops,
following the lead of Colonel Henry Tucker, had
devoted thought to the problem of import and had
hit upon a method of securing immunity from seizure
by juggling with papers and titles. They cleared to
St. Eustatia (or presumably St. Thomas), made their
vessels partly Dutch (or Danish) property, traded as
neutrals to the French islands for a time; then hoisted
their original colors, proceeded to St. Kitts, obtained
correct clearances from obliging officials like the one
at Sandy Cove and returned to Bermuda in patriotic
guise, having done business with neutral, rebel,
enemy and friend alike. The device could be worked
as well for commerce with the northern states. Some
Bermudians cleared for Halifax, made sales to or
exchanges with their American friends in the Bay of
Fundy and secured clearances for return from William
Johnstone the complaisant customs collector of Liver-
pool. So had developed a traffic with New England;
and twelve to fourteen Bermudian sail had furnished
salt through Boston to the French army and fleet in
Newport. There remained some danger from the keen
privateers of New England; but even this difficulty
had been overcome by certain merchants, Britons by
birth and resident in Bermuda. They cleared vessels
for Nova Scotia and addressed them to merchants in
Boston in case of capture, thereby securing the services of the privateers as escorts. It was reported also
that these Britons had money at interest with the
legislature of Massachusetts, considering the war

nothing more than an incidental risk in their business relations with Americans.[13]

But many Bermudians scorned these devious ways and continued a direct traffic with the continent, taking their chances with privateers and men of war. "Vessels have passed and repassed continually to the colonies in rebellion," wrote the lieutenant-governor, "esteeming it a mere speculation and only the loss of their property if taken," i.e. not an unpatriotic act. At the end of December 1780, six Bermudian sail were at Ocrecock, North Carolina, and many in other inlets along the coast. "The perfection they bring their vessels to makes them outsail all cruisers" and their artifices enabled them to elude the customs officers. "A week scarce passes but vessels return from the rebels; boats able to live in almost any sea go out the moment a vessel can be discerned, smuggle in cargoes, carry off rebel prisoners and carry on a correspondence with the rebels." In one short period in the early months of 1781, by Bruere's reckoning, twenty sloops and schooners had escaped the customs.[14] In June 1781 Tudor Hinson and Captain Dickson arrived home from a voyage to North Carolina. Bruere took up their conduct with the council; that body, however, found the intent of the two Bermudians honest but their procedure to blame since they should have asked the lieutenant-governor's permission to enter and unload. Thus two prominent suspects escaped.[15] It was clear that in 1780-1781 Bermudian commerce with the enemy had grown by

[13] George Bruere to Germain, December 12, 1780, January 7 and March 26, 1781; Brimage to Germain, undated 1780. All cited above.
[14] George Bruere to Germain, December 12, 1780, January 7, February 8, and March 26, 1781, all in C. O. 37 vol. 38.
[15] Council minutes of June 20, 1781, in C. O. 40 vol. 18.

leaps and bounds, far exceeding the limits of a mere importation of provisions and apparently little impeded by the revocation of the favors of the Continental Congress. In 1782, by Surgeon Richard Bell's estimate, the Bermudians were wealthy from trade and were enduring fewer hardships than any other of the islanders of the New World.[16]

The young lieutenant-governor had made his first undertaking to Germain that the trade with the rebels should be no more; and courageously he set about his task, fully realizing that he was coping with a hydra-headed monster. He wrote to all the British commanders on the continent to watch the Bermudians, warning them about the artifices "of which they are the most complete masters . . . by getting over most oaths, making the most loyal professions at home though at the same time acting diametrically opposite to them here" and especially about their practice of securing double papers to carry on a forced trade. The aid to American prisoners he could easily circumvent by exchanging the men with the Americans, taking receipts in return. Meanwhile he instigated the customs officers to new efforts; but these found that usually before they could catch sloops with contraband the wily crews had landed most or all of the cargoes. For want of an armed vessel the officers were well nigh helpless. Accordingly he fitted out a boat which had been taken by the *Galatea*, put her in charge of Lieutenant David Davis of the garrison battalion and used her in aid of customs at the west end. He sent an officer and fifteen soldiers there also and thus arranged for combined land and sea operations. Suspecting the pilots of that area to be in

[16] Richard Bell to "Dear Colonel" (unidentified), July 12, 1782, in C. O. 37 vol. 38.

conspiracy with the smugglers, he discharged them and set soldiers in charge of the pilotage. These efforts soon bore fruit; in January six or seven vessels, owned chiefly by members of the assembly, were taken. But when a sloop was captured, difficulties were by no means at an end. The *Paragon*, owned by the Tuckers at the Bridge, came thus into the toils of the law; but Henry of Somerset and his gang smuggled one incriminating witness off the island, intimidated another and in the ensuing absence of evidence obtained an interlocutory decree for the discharge of the vessel.[17] In this case the best efforts of lieutenant-governor and customs officers were baffled; but in others they were more fortunate. In the spring Bruere caught three men, one on his fourth trip to Boston; he discharged two as insignificant and kept the other in jail as a spy.[18] In the summer a Boston trader arrived under false papers with lumber and exchanged it for salt from one John Todd, a Scotsman of St. Georges who had been at Boston three or four times and was a member of the anti-privateering association. Bruere saw through the pretense and arrested Todd in spite of the latter's attempt to escape in an open boat to a vessel bound for Turks Islands. Bascome tried to rescue his friend by a *habeas corpus*; but here Bruere easily baffled him. The lieutenant-governor would have pardoned the man if he had confessed his fault, which he refused to do by Bascome's advice; and in default of penitence apparently sent him to New York for trial. Meanwhile Bruere realized that he had increased his difficulties by an error. On his arrival he had allowed

[17] George Bruere to Germain, January 7, 1781, January 15, February 8, March 26, 1781, all in C. O. 37 vol. 38.

[18] George Bruere to Ben Thompson, July 15, 1781, in C. O. 37 vol. 38.

the controller Copeland Stiles to persuade him to permit vessels entry to the country ports on condition that their masters should report in person to St. Georges and settle with customs. Bermudian honesty was not equal to such a test; but he postponed a recall of the order in the hope of inducing the assembly to vote money for the forts. Deciding that the hope was vain, in March 1781 he commanded all vessels whether inbound or outbound to call at St. Georges and submit to search. For the enforcement of his several orders he had at his disposal only the converted prize, the soldiers and the customs staff. He endeavored to secure a vessel of the navy; and finally in August 1781 procured the *Hornet* which proved another *Nautilus* and speedily drove the smugglers to cover.[19] His greatest triumph, however, was in outwitting Henry Tucker of Somerset, frustrating two attempted voyages of the *Friendship*. "Informations were then particularly encouraged and in spite of every precaution were found to take effect," wrote the surprised Henry later.[20] By the autumn of 1781 George Bruere had not abolished the trade in contraband but he had considerably reduced it, spreading dismay among his opponents. His success exasperated the mariner smugglers and quite wore through their last shreds of loyalty. Some of them, viewing the privileges accorded by the French to the inhabitants of the captured West India islands, desired a similar status of practical neutrality and solicited from Washington the favor of an invasion. The appeal was at least a measure of the effectiveness of Bruere's policy.

[19] George Bruere to Germain, February 8, March 26, October 17, 1781, in C. O. 37 vol. 38. The Boston trader was the *Porgy*, mentioned below, p. 116.
[20] Henry Tucker of Somerset to St. George, February 19, 1785. T. H. P.

In his task of driving wilful and obstinate Bermudians into the narrow way, the lieutenant-governor was obliged to devise a policy with regard to the legislature. He hoped to persuade them to alter their ways, to meet regularly and to compel dilatory committees to take action; then to grapple seriously with neglected business, to provide police, encourage agriculture, set order in their financial proceedings and undertake certain public works much overdue like the repair of Government House, of the ferry bridges and the landings on both sides of the ferry. He had also a military program; he desired the assembly to provide funds for fortifications, for new barracks and for the hospital already promised and to permit the soldiers to fish by modifying certain existing laws. But above all he longed to convert the members from their unpatriotic ways, from their indulgence in illicit trade and their refusal to privateer. This he hoped to do by exhortation or reproach in his messages to them.

He commenced by communicating to the council a letter from Germain which urged that as the troops were in Bermuda to protect the inhabitants, the legislature should find quarters for them and compensate the owners of the houses they had occupied.[21] The assembly had been adjourned to January 29; but in accord with its peculiar traditions it did not meet until February 1. The lieutenant-governor had ready a glowing address. He urged the members to attend to the necessary public works, to build barracks for the troops and to honor their debts, it being notorious that they did not pay salaries to their own clerks. Then he resumed the topic which he had most at heart. They protested themselves loyal subjects, why

[21] Minutes of executive council, January 9, 1781. (Bermuda Archives.)

did they not act at such? Why did they continue to sell salt to the rebels and buy tobacco from them? "Let us not deceive ourselves . . . [liberty] is no-where to be found as pure and unadulterated as under our limited monarchy. It flies committees, illegal meetings, proscriptions, combinations . . . stray not after it to rebel states and new-fangled systems! In Britain and under British government you will find it; there the laws rule and no man is to arrogate to himself powers he is not constitutionally invested with. . . ." He exhorted the assemblymen and no doubt Bermudians in general, to fit out privateers and combine patriotism with profits. "Imagine not you can act with impunity the detestable double part of subjects to Britain and friends to her enemies!"[22]

The eloquence, however, moved the stiff-necked men of the legislature no farther than to a small concession which would not interfere with business. They resolved to permit the troops to use the new jail as a barrack, attended to some minor matters and requested an adjournment, which was granted. They met again on March 15 and heard a message void of controversy, Bruere perhaps hoping to encourage any slight tendency to cooperation. The hope was not altogether vain, for apparently half of the members present desired to follow the lieutenant-governor's lead while the other half, presumably under Henry Tucker of Somerset's direction, cast about for ways and means of resistance. The consequence was a series of contradictory actions. On the one hand the assembly resolved to devote £500 of its new surplus to barracks and fortifications, £100 to the hospital,

[22] George Bruere to Germain, February 8, 1781, cited above; minutes of assembly, February 1, 1781, in C. O. 40 vol. 18.

£300 to Mrs. Bruere.[23] On the other hand it passed a
bill "absurd and contradictory" intended if Bruere's
surmise was correct to procure for the lower house
control of the fund arising from a tax on gunpowder.
The bill of course was refused by the council. Henry
Tucker's party also secured passage of two resolves,
one censuring the late governor for applying to works
and fortifications some £200 out of the powder fund,
the other condemning George Bruere's action in using
£40 of that fund toward finishing the governor's
house and the town guardhouse; but the party of
compromise were able to prevent these from reaching
the council. After the adjournment, Bruere inspected
the minutes of the lower house, found these resolves
and discovered references to a correspondence with
Colonel Henry Tucker involving assemblymen and
two councillors (Chief Justice Burch and Henry
Tucker, Jr.) which in plain violation of constitutional
usage, had not been communicated to the rest of the
council or to himself. He observed also that the
assembly had voted £750, over and above £2000
previously paid, to the salary of Colonel Henry
Tucker while leaving unpaid the balance (£1500) due
to the late governor and the salaries of the clergymen; and in wrath he viewed the grant to fortifications as a niggardly pittance.[24] He contained his
sentiments for the time; but as summer drew on, he
found that the committees in charge of the funds
voted for military purposes evaded action by con-
tinual adjournments. At the same time his captures

[23] The minutes of executive council of March 17, 1781 (Bermuda Archives)
mention £450 voted for military purposes exclusive of the hospital. I have
preferred Bruere's figures.

[24] George Bruere to Germain, March 26, 1781, cited above; assembly
minutes, March 15-22, 1781, in C.O. 40 vol. 18.

of illicit traders and the incident of Hinson and Dickson proved that his offer of the previous October to overlook past sins if no new were committed, had been disregarded.

When the assembly met again therefore on June 19, he was ready with another sermon of hot reproach. He recapitulated the misdeeds of the islanders; the election and despatch of delegates to Congress, the theft of the powder "with the assistance and the privity" of many of the inhabitants, the trade with the Americans, the still general refusal to privateer. "To what state have wicked designing men brought these isles . . . they have caused a misguided and deluded people to do all they could to serve the Americans! Have not those who dared oppose their diabolical system been threatened, abused, oppressed, associated against and has not the law even been perverted to aid those ends?" He denounced "the illegal meetings and risings in force to compel British privateers to give up their legally captured Bermuda vessels or to oblige Crown officers to relinquish their duty." He pointed out the ruinous condition of Government House and of the public offices, the wretchedness of the police, the depredations of the idle who preferred theft to labor, the smuggling by the Danish islands, the clipping of coins, the sloth of the committees on fortifications; and in conclusion he suggested a tax on labor and materials in each parish.[25]

The assembly writhed under the lash but could not escape a feeling of guilt. Henry Tucker of Somerset drew up a reply in a tone of subdued protest which he conceived suitable to the occasion. Once more he employed the well worn camouflage "we, His Majes-

[25] Assembly minutes, June 19, 1781, in C. O. 40 vol. 18.

ty's most loyal and dutiful subjects" and hinted at opposition by asserting that the freedom of the British Empire "is universally acknowledged to extend beyond that of any government whatever." He declared "most seriously and religiously that the people of these islands are now and ever have been throughout the whole of the present unhappy commotions in America, however they may have been otherwise represented or appearances may have militated against them, entirely at the peace of His Majesty." That the humor of such statements had by now quite evaporated probably did not escape Henry, who judged them still useful as dust in the eyes of the loyal. He assured the lieutenant-governor that the assemblymen would conduct themselves in the way most conducive to the real service of His Majesty and the security and welfare of the islands which was "ever more effectually promoted by conciliatory than by inflammatory measures." This labored attempt to continue the bluff, flavored with phrases of rebuke, did not really do justice to Henry's ingenuity. In response Bruere went straight to the main point and declared that since his arrival more than twenty sail of vessels had come home from trading with the Americans, some of them owned by members of the house. To this specific accusation the assembly could make no reply.[26]

Uneasy under the pressure, the members made more concessions. They resolved to repair the barracks at the ferry, pushed a new law about the militia and asked the lieutenant-governor to order the J. P.'s of each parish to convene the inhabitants and exhort them to prepare for defense. They also voted to rent

[26] Minutes of assembly, June 20-23, 1781, in C. O. 40 vol. 18.

a house for three months "for Governor William Browne" who had been appointed but had not arrived; the wording being doubtless Henry Tucker's method of taking a slap at Bruere. Ignoring the phrase, the lieutenant-governor had a right to feel that his efforts had not been wholly unsuccessful.[27]

Until this time he had little definite information about the activities of Colonel Henry Tucker in London. But early in July 1781, some letters from that worthy, dated the previous year and addressed to Henry Tucker of Somerset and George Bascome, came into his hands; they had been forwarded from Boston by John Hancock in the spurious flag of truce *Porgy*. These communications expressed fear about George Bruere's policies, hopes that young Traill would persuade his father to take the Bermudian point of view, advice to make concessions to the ministry and sundry personal matters; nothing exactly treasonous but a good deal which confirmed Bruere's suspicions of the agent.[28] A governor more given to subtle ways might have used the letters to effect a politic blackmail on the leaders of the assembly. But George Bruere's straightforwardness permitted him no such thought. When on August 16 he met the assembly again, his wrath had not abated a jot. In another message of hot challenge and rebuke he denounced the intrigues "to palliate and cover the intercourse between these islands and America," the solicitation by the agent of places for himself and his friends, the attempt to create friction in the administration and to pervert Traill, the attack

[27] Minutes of assembly, June 20-23, 1781, cited above.
[28] Colonel Henry Tucker to George Bascome, August 8, 1780, and to Henry Tucker of Somerset, August 8 and September 30, 1780, in C. O. 37 vol. 38.

on the lieutenant-governor himself. "My record is clear," proclaimed the young executive proudly if indiscreetly; "your records for fifty years show vilification of the governor by the factious" whenever these failed to obtain their objects. From reproaches he turned to urge a radical alteration in Bermudian habits. Let them not think that the administration would be duped into creating several ports of entry for the convenience of smugglers; let the traders gather together into towns and others avail themselves of their own soil. "Fortunate it would be for Bermuda if the country were left to culture and the merchants established here; but contrary to the general good, every man from private interest strives to have the town contiguous to his own estate. . . . Imitate Barbados; throw your vales into cultivation; they will yield abundantly and will return much greater profit than the growth of timber." Bermudians had formerly exported corn and tobacco; why did they not do so now? In conclusion came a reprimand about finances; why did they pay the agent £500 a year, more than the most opulent West India island allowed, when debts, Government House, fortifications clamored for attention? This message was followed by another on August 17 to insist on necessary military measures. The house bowed to the storm, disclaimed desire to enter an argument and replied noncommittally.[29] Presently they were adjourned to September 18. All the while Henry Tucker of Somerset felt himself a marked man and lay low "under a disagreeable restraint."[30] So cleverly had he covered his tracks, however, that no positive evidence could be got against him.

[29] Minutes of assembly, August 16-17, 1781, in C. O. 40 vol. 18.
[30] Henry Tucker of Somerset to St. George, August 9, 1781. T. H. P.

The day before that appointed for the next sitting, Cornelius Hinson, speaker of the house, wrote to Bruere pleading illness and asking for a further prorogation until October. The council was inclined to support the request. But Bruere would brook no delay. He expressed regret for the speaker's indisposition but insisted on the necessity of a session to deal with public business, at the same time rebuking the practice of sending private letters on public matters from individuals of either legislative body as "derogatory, unconstitutional, irregular."[31] The legislature therefore met on September 20; and in response to more messages about quarters and provisions for the troops, voted an additional £250. But the Tucker faction was planning a broadside; and at the end of a week they induced the members present to send up an address drawn up probably by Henry Tucker of Somerset and George Bascome.[31a]

For the sake of peace, they asserted, they had hitherto given way to "that high hand your Honor has affected to hold over all our public proceedings rather improperly." This they had done from hope that Governor Browne's arrival would fix a period to that "(your Honor will be pleased to excuse the expression) motley and unconstitutional government which . . . has been generally administered from the first moment of your Honor's accession to command within these islands, for which no plea can be urged in justification as the peace of His Majesty in the most extensive sense of the word uninterruptedly prevailed among the people." The clandestine trade which had originated in necessity had, they claimed,

---

[31] Minutes of executive council, September 17, 1781. (Bermuda Archives.)

[31a] It is to be presumed that most of the members favorable to Bruere had gone home, leaving a clear field to Henry Tucker's group.

declined; his rebukes were therefore undeserved.[31b] "In anxious expectation of a change, we should yet have forborne a public stricture on those proceedings but for the continued goadings of your Honor; reproach having been added to reproach and insult having succeeded to insult." To keep silent then would mean to admit the charges. The irregularities on which he had harped had not originated in a traitorous design; there was in Bermuda the most positive and unaffected attachment of the people to their sovereign, the constitution and the laws. Indeed the present house had gone to a previously unknown length to accommodate the troops. In the accusations against Colonel Henry Tucker, Bruere had departed from strict attention to the truth; he must have known that the gentleman had undertaken the duty with reluctance, that he had received recognition as agent by ministers in London, that he still had the approval of assembly and people. "The terrible schemes, plots and combinations" revealed in the letters "will after every exertion of your Honor in support of the pompous description given to the public unavoidably end as the story of the mountain and the mouse." They accused him of sacrificing the dignity of his office by prying into the letters. In conclusion they expressed their trust in His Majesty "ever attentive to the grievances of his subjects" and their own "anxious and unfeigned wishes in which we are most heartily joined by the people at large, for the arrival of Governor Browne from whose general character we are led to expect more temperate proceedings and a satisfaction in the conduct of public business which has been totally inexperienced under the administra-

[31b] An instance of Henry Tucker of Somerset's peculiar type of humor.

tion of your Honor." Apart from the censure which of course was deliberately calculated to annoy, the message is merely another manifestation of the policy of bluff and can have deceived very few in the year 1781. Henry Tucker of Somerset and George Bascome were masters in the art of lying without the flutter of an eyelash.

The hard words need not really have disturbed George Bruere, springing as they obviously did from a sense of defeat on the part of the Tucker group. But for a person of his temperament, coolness was a difficult virtue. Thrown into fury, he replied at once to the "wanton abuse and unsubstantiated calumnious allegations . . . [which] cannot but redound to the disgrace of the leading members that framed it." The intercourse with the Americans was not, as falsely alleged, for provisions but for needless commodities. The notorious misdeeds of the last six years "called for the utmost exertion to warn a deluded people of their misleaders." He recalled to the members his offer on arrival to forget the past if the disaffected should return to duty, an offer made in vain. He challenged anyone to prove that laws were impeded or justice not done. He called on his assailants to make definite charges and produce proofs. Their personal attacks, lavished on every governor of Bermuda, "he who has spent a life in honor is above and heartily despises." The Tucker letters had been opened only in accord with the rules of war. "Every paragraph in the assembly's address is strictly the reverse of truth," he concluded. He then dissolved the assembly and ordered elections, however little promise that course might seem to hold.[32]

[32] Minutes of assembly September 27-29, 1781, in C. O. 40 vol. 18: complaint of council and assembly to Crown, July 29, 1782, cited above. The

In the meantime, if the lieutenant-governor's surmise was correct, Henry Tucker of Somerset's group
adopted the policy suggested by Colonel Henry, of
fomenting strife among the officers of administration.
Mr. Palmer the new attorney-general fell foul of the
commanding officer and received a reprimand from
him. He next quarrelled with Cazneau and insulted
him on the parade. Last, he took to criticizing
Bruere's measures in court. Bruere asked him to come
privately and make complaints of any actions he
thought wrong; and on his failure to do so while
persisting in his conduct, suspended him and gave
his place pro tempore to the same Graham who had
occupied it before. Next occurred friction with the
customs officials. Joseph Laborn, searcher at the west
end, neglected his duty to the extent of provoking
complaints from the soldiers who assisted him.
Bruere suspended him and appointed in his room
Paul Bascome who had well proved his loyalty at
Turks Islands.[33] Robert Traill the customs collector
did not object to the removal of Laborn but refused
to admit Bruere's authority to appoint, till threatened
with suspension. Soon Traill became involved in
a quarrel with Lieutenant Davis of the government boat over a brigantine from Boston seized first

complaint states further that Bruere signed warrants for the arrest of two
members, called out the troops and surrounded the assembly; but was balked
by the commanding officer who decided that he had no power to act. But
Pendock Neale unreservedly denies this assertion, declaring that if Bruere
had done such a thing, he (Neale) could not but have known it. (Deposition
of March 10, 1784, in C. O. 37 vol. 27.) In any conflict of statement with
Henry Tucker of Somerset and George Bascome, Neale, from his honesty has
the right of way.

[33] Laborn had once been clerk in the collector's office; he is described as
small in size (Mrs. Henry Tucker, Jr., to St. George, June 15, 1772; Paul
Bascome's loyalty, in Henry Tucker, Sr., to St. George, October 15, 1778.
T. H. P.).

by Traill but claimed by Davis; and Bruere took the side of Davis. Until this time the lieutenant-governor had cultivated Traill in accord with directions from home, paying him "as much attention as a father," placing his servants and table at the collector's command and ignoring "many unaccountable incivilities." But now good relations ceased and Traill opposed the lieutenant-governor in council on matters agreed on previously between them in private, even cancelling the purchase of a smack to aid against the smugglers. Finally Traill, perhaps under the influence of Controller Stiles, took it on himself to allow persons and letters to leave the *Porgy* under a flag of truce and thereby incurred a rebuke from the captain of the troops in charge of inspection. High words followed at table, Traill and his son behaved "in the most insolent manner" and went off. Traill now ranged himself on the side of the opposition in the September session of the assembly and openly declared his friendship with Henry Tucker of Somerset, dining with him on the day of the provocative address. At this turn of events the Tucker group, recently despondent, became jubilant, proclaiming that if they could have the collector on their side, they cared not who was governor. Bruere attributed the falling away of Palmer and Traill to the wiles of George Bascome; and for once he gave way to discouragement, wishing to leave the island for the East Indies or South America. The council was a broken reed, containing "so strong a connection" as to outvote him on any material point; and he felt he could make no more changes in it. Even after his great efforts the loyalty of the inhabitants was far from perfect: "I'm grieved to think many of the people are so disaffected that they would rather invite than repel an enemy." But he soon found heart again and resumed his pressure on the sluggard and reluctant of the islanders.[34]

He met the theoretically new assembly on November 15 with a speech short but fierce, defying "new leagues and old associations" denouncing "rebel traders with matchless effrontery [who] dare avow and pretend to justify their traitorous intercourse" and reiterating the purity of his aims "whatever the wicked may suggest." Whether converted, subdued or merely lying in wait, the assembly did not reply in kind; and succeeding exchanges became comparatively amicable. He pressed for repair of Government House, for an allowance to himself in lieu of servants (as to other governors), for relief of scarcity by privateering, trade with reconquered Georgia, agriculture and a good police, for payment for repairs at the Castle and Fort Paget and defensive works elsewhere, notably at Brackish Pond. As usual the assembly found the list excessive but did vote money for fortifications including repairs to guns in Devonshire.[35] The concession was probably the maximum that could be expected.

At last Bruere could find some consolation; for his efforts had stirred a real response. In April Warwick parish had stated in a petition that its inhabitants were ready to oppose any attack by the enemies of Great Britain and required only guns, powder and a commander.[36] More remarkable, some of the islanders joined Goodrich in fitting out another privateer. Others set about preparing more; and by October

[34] George Bruere to Germain, October 17, and to Ben Thompson, October 19, 1781, in C. O. 37 vol. 38.

[35] Minutes of assembly and council, November 15-17, 1781, in C. O. 37 vol. 38.

[36] Minutes of executive council, April 21, 1781 (Bermuda Archives); also in C. O. 40 vol. 18, a better version.

half a dozen of the swiftest sloops were ready to spoil enemy commerce. The lieutenant-governor noted the change with pleasure, limited though it was to a part of the inhabitants; and he felt sure that if it were not for the influence of the Tucker faction, most people would equip vessels against the Americans instead of assisting them by way of the Danish islands. Having failed to obtain from the assembly a modification of the law about fish nurseries, he took that law into his own hands and permitted the soldiers to violate it for the sake of food. He pressed the construction of works and barracks in spite of all obstacles thrown in his way by sloth or malice; and by mid-December the magazines were finished, the hospital, the barracks and other works approaching the stage of completion.[37] In face of these accomplishments it was a comparative trifle that he had to advance his own money for the upkeep of the government boats. It is a fair conjecture that given a longer term and better support from home, George Bruere would have paralyzed the opposition and brought most of the Bermudians around to some degree of positive loyalty.

[37] George Bruere to Germain October 17 and December 15, 1781. C. O. 37 vol. 38. The development of privateering in 1782 and 1783 was attributed by many Bermudians "to the lieutenant-governor's exertions and encouragement." Deposition of Neale, March 10, 1784, cited above. The new privateers were manned chiefly by seaman out of a job from George Bruere's suppression of illicit trade, who thereby manifested their high impartiality toward the belligerents.

CHAPTER VII

GOVERNOR WILLIAM BROWNE

LORD GEORGE GERMAIN had sent out George Bruere to effect a reformation in Bermuda which to the best of his ability the latter had done. For obscure reasons, however, the secretary changed his policy. He had indeed once approved Bruere's "industry and zeal" but in the same breath had informed him that he was sending a governor to relieve him, William Browne who had been a judge of the supreme court of Boston. All summer of 1781 while Bruere coped resolutely with his difficulties, Germain could not spare even these few words of praise. When instructing Browne about his conduct, he informed him of Bruere's drastic measures, hoped that these would produce a salutary effect and advised in their place a policy of conciliation. Browne would restore the persons ejected from their posts, announce the abolition of the governor's fees on whales and win over the principal inhabitants.[1] The adoption of this policy of entire surrender to the makers of trouble shows how little Germain cared about affairs in Bermuda in spite of all the official despatches.[1a]

With some hint of these intentions having preceded him, Browne reached Bermuda on December 16, 1781. He met "a great reception from all ranks" and especially from Councillor Henry Tucker, Jr., whom

[1] Germain to George Bruere, February 7, 1781; to Browne, June 30, 1781, in C. O. 37 vol. 38; Board of Trade to Browne, June 12, 1781, in C. O. 38 vol. 10. There is a sketch of Browne in *Dictionary of American Biography*, III, pp. 169-70.

[1a] An obvious guess is that the machinations of Colonel Henry effected the change in Germain's policy: but I can find nothing positive in support of this view.

he presently appointed to the post of acting secretary and provost marshal.[2] All gave him their positive assurances that the assembly would bring "the best dispositions." Basking in this popularity, he restored Burch to the office of chief justice "which I think he deserves" and gave back their commissions to the deposed field officers of the militia. He did not restore Palmer or Laborn, suspended after his instructions had been made out, and he preferred to retain Graham as attorney-general. To the inhabitants at large he announced the concession about fees and thereby earned great approval.

While applause attended Browne, curses followed his predecessor. The opposition proceeded to take revenge and commenced an action of trespass in King's Bench against Bruere. Burch, back on the bench, despatched the lieutenant-governor to jail; but the latter secured bail and sailed promptly for England while Traill worked off his spleen in an "infamous and scurrilous placard." The council and assembly pursued the fallen executive with an address to the King in May 1782 and a formal complaint in July, summing up his acts to strengthen imperial authority. He replied by charging Jones, Hunt, Burch, Harvey, Tucker, Tudor, Traill, members at one time or another of the council, with their part in the revenue law of September 23, 1780, in the use of funds to pay the agent instead of to secure the health of the troops in the anti-privateering association; and he had easily the best of the argument.[3]

Browne met the assembly in May 1782. It "showed

[2] In accord with instructions; Colonel Henry had arranged the appointment in London.

[3] Browne to Germain, January 12, 1782; council and assembly of Bermuda to Crown, July 29, 1782; Bruere's reply undated. All in C. O. 37 vol. 38.

a good spirit," thanked His Majesty for encouraging the whale fishery and displayed a general "warmth of gratitude." A year later he reported a model lower house which was praying His Majesty to establish a free port, a prayer which islanders had long anticipated by works. He remarked on "the harmony which has happily subsisted among the several branches of the legislature ever since I had the honor to preside over it."[4] His feeling of satisfaction was fully reciprocated; even that person of fastidious taste in governors, Henry Tucker of Somerset, expressed himself as perfectly pleased with Browne.[5] The harmony which Browne reported certainly existed but it was of the sort which prevails between the lion and the lamb inside. The governor had delivered himself and the administration entirely to the dominant clique of the island.

These now turned their attention to the relics of George Bruere's government. The west enders developed nice scruples about submitting to search by Paul Bascome, taking Traill's view that he had been appointed illegally. They met Bascome's efforts with acts of violence until on the assembly's address, Browne removed him and gave his place to another.[6] George Bascome now seized an opportunity for a blow at one of Bruere's principal supports. When the former garrison of Rattan had arrived at Bermuda on exchange from Havana, Major Anstruther mustered them with the Royal Grenadiers under his own command, although he had no official account of them. The "rebel lawyer" persuaded one of these men

[4] Browne to Germain, May 16, 1782; to Townshend, April 30, 1783 (two letters), in C. O. 37 vol. 38.
[5] Henry Tucker of Somerset to St. George, May 30, 1786. T. H. P.
[6] Browne to Earl of Shelburne, February 15, 1783, in C. O. 37 vol. 38.

to secure from the governor and council a *habeas corpus* on the ground that the major was depriving him of liberty.[7] Such an act threatened the major's control of the newly arrived men although these did not take advantage of it. Surgeon Richard Bell while acknowledging the erection of the hospital at Bruere's impulse, wrote of the assembly as "lost to humanity as to every loyal sentiment and feeling," when left by themselves to deal with the troops. Illicit trade hardly troubled Browne, eliciting from him once a suggestion to circumvent it by importation from Great Britain.[8] The inference is that the governor was well hoodwinked by his islanders.

In one respect, however, the controlling circle altered their policy. Finding that Congress now classed them as enemies and would not alter its policy for any intrigues or prayers, they took revenge by relaxing their opposition to privateering as Colonel Henry Tucker had long urged them to do. Browne realized with pleasure that his islanders were taking to that pursuit with some zeal, having captured thirty-four prizes in the period from January 1 to April 30, 1782. By January 1782 the new occupation had become almost popular. The people, wrote Traill, "now discover a spirit that fully convinces they are at this period no friends to the Americans; for the fitting out of privateers in all parts of the islands in order to annoy their trade is become so general that there are now about eighteen sail commissioned and belonging to it." From January 5 to September 19,

---

[7] Major W. Anstruther to "Dear Sir," unidentified, April 15, 1783, in C. O. 37 vol. 38.

[8] Bell to "Dear Colonel," July 12, 1782; Browne to Germain, January 12, 1782, cited above.

1782, ninety-three prizes were brought in.[9] Though George Bruere was gone, his policy in this respect had at last obtained success, as Cazneau and Graham may have informed him when they too quitted Bermuda in the spring of 1783.

The practice of privateering, however, was certain to incur a breach of the friendly relations which had existed officially and unofficially between the Americans and the controlling clique of Bermuda since 1775. In the autumn of 1781 when George Bruere had brought illicit trade to straits, four individuals (Thomas Roberts, Thomas Morgan, Ben Stiles, James Briggs) invited Washington to invade the island, if necessary with the aid of the French, assuring him that the inhabitants were too well disposed to shake off the tyranny of Britain to make any opposition to the allies of America and suggesting a capitulation on the terms accorded Grenada, providing for neutrality while the war lasted.[10] At the same time J. M. Varnum was writing to Washington arguing in favor of such a project that the inhabitants of Bermuda were in general friendly to the United States and dependent on them for subsistence; he claimed that five hundred men and three or four frigates could seize the islands. In August 1782 when the situation on the continent had made such schemes more feasible, a plan of invasion in cooperation with

[9] Browne to Germain, May 16, 1782; Robert Traill to Shelburne, January 4 and September 19, 1782, in C. O. 37 vol. 38.

[10] The four to Washington, October 23, 1781, in T. H. P.; they evidently sent the letter by St. George Tucker. I must add that Dr. Wilkinson is in some doubt whether the four were Bermudians. He considers it possible that their names, although appended, were not signatures but formed a list of pilots available for an expedition.

The names, however, seem Bermudian, particularly Morgan and Stiles: and that an invitation was sent to Washington appears from the letter of Major Anstruther, mentioned below.

the French fleet was mooted in Congress.[11] Though nothing came of these proposals, perhaps because of the restored British supremacy at sea, word of them reached the island. Major Anstruther in alarm wrote that an attack was imminent, invited by some of the natives who had agreed to give up Bermuda if the Americans should come in force. In fact American armed vessels hung around Bermuda all summer, taking privateers and other ships in sight of land. But most Bermudians had now committed themselves to a more loyal course. In May Browne and his legislature were busy with projects of defense, repairing forts, attending to artillery and purchasing ammunition. The militia did some training in the summer, though in need of arms, powder and ball. Colonel Henry Tucker was sure that if the enemy came, the inhabitants would resist in a way befitting "as loyal subjects as any in His Majesty's dominions" although his authority on loyalty was not of the best.[12] Bermuda and the United States were at last approaching a state of hostilities. But the next year brought a general peace; and the Bermudians settled down to their old ways of life, neglecting the land and seeking the seas for a livelihood.

The conclusion from the standpoint of the dominant element of the island was expressed by George Bascome. "In the midst of this mighty struggle for glory, dominion and liberty, poor little Bermuda has observed a strict neutrality. This perhaps you will say was the most difficult political manoeuvre that could be attempted. Be it so; God be thanked; the

[11] Letters to members of the Continental Congress, VI, 230 and 422.

[12] Browne to Germain, May 8, 1782; Henry Tucker, Sr., to E. Nepean, October 30, 1782, and to Thos. Townshend, November 30, 1782, in C. O. 37 vol. 38.

lives of 14,000 souls have been saved by it."[13] The statement was hardly accurate, Bermudian relations with the States from 1775 to 1782 having been those of an ally rather than a neutral; but it indicates what most of the controlling group imagined they were doing. Though sharers in the colonial life of North America, the islanders lived to themselves sufficiently to stifle any spark of American nationality. On the part neither of the dominant circle nor of the mass of inhabitants was there any desire to revolt against imperial authority, interested professions to Congress notwithstanding. Many humble Bermudians had retained some instinct of positive loyalty even in the censorious eyes of George Bruere. But the leading merchants and shipowners had conceived it desirable to maintain if possible the same economic relations with the continental colonies in war as in peace. They had therefore led Bermuda into a passive conflict with the mother country and an association with the Americans which carried Bermuda closest of all the non-revolutionary colonies to the thirteen which separated from the Empire. In the end the refugee privateers and George Bruere had compelled the abandonment of the policy; and Bermuda remained under the British flag.[13a]

[13] To St. George Tucker, March 28, 1778, in T. H. P.

[13a] George Bruere died in the autumn of 1785, weakened by his wounds and his service. Henry Tucker, Jr., to St. George, January 1, 1786, in T.H.P. His epitaph might well be the words of Neale: "He certainly by his conduct public and private manifested the most fervent and disinterested zeal for the good of his King and country and the credit of Bermuda." Deposition of March 10, 1784, cited above.

APPENDIX I

THE ENQUIRY ABOUT THE POWDER IN 1786

IN February 1786 the loyal party in the Bermuda assembly raised the question of the theft of the powder again and secured a committee of enquiry composed of members of both houses. This committee received a communication from Ben Williams of Brackish Pond, justice of Devonshire and staunch loyalist, relating a conversation he had had with Joseph Jennings at the Flats, his wife's father. Jennings had informed him about the approach made to him by James Tucker for his boat for the purpose of the robbery, as we have described above. Now Joseph Jennings himself sent in a paper confirming the facts related by Williams. Such evidence would certainly seem enough for an enquiry; but the committee, persons of the dominant clique, were determined not to pursue it and declared the information too frivolous and nugatory for notice. They reported so to the council which unanimously accepted their verdict, and to the assembly which debated the matter. The loyalists objected to the report but were overruled, 16 to 10. Jennings then applied to the assembly to have his deposition taken, but this also was refused. The loyal ten were Harry Jacobs (leader), David Sears, Richard Peniston, Joseph Richardson, Anthony Gilbert, Sam Williams, R. Steed, B. Cox, Thomas Newson[1], William Dunscomb. Thus the enquiry was stifled and the theft of the powder remained a mystery. (Henry Tucker, Sr., to St. George, April 19, 1786, in T. H. P.; minutes of assembly, February 11 to March 21, 1786.)

[1] Also spelled Nusum, probably Newsome. Most of the ten were newcomers to the assembly.

INDEX

Adelphi, sloop hired by Tuckers, 55-7

Anstruther, Major William, garrison commander: appointed to council, 102; fears attack on island, 130; hampered by George Bascome, 127-8

Assembly of Bermuda: affair of Salt Kettle, 76-7; appeal to King, 78; appeal to Lord Howe, 77-8; appointment of agent, 93-4; attempt to renew embargo, 79; attitude toward theft of powder, 50-1; bickering with Bruere 1776-77, 75-80; complaints of about the troops suppressing contraband trade, 93; composition, 17; dispute over ports of entry, 25-6, 29-30; division over George Bruere's appeal for patriotic policies and ensuing bickering, 111-23; embargo on export of food in May 1775, 43; enquiry about theft of powder, 133; exceptions to embargo, 63; expiration of embargo and failure of renewal, 66; friction with Bruere in 1780, 96-7; indifference of members to attendance, 17-18; protests against the suppression of contraband by vessels of Royal Navy, 73-8; quarrel with council and Bruere 1769-72, 30-6; question of resident candidates, 29-30; reception of Governor Bruere 1764, 24; renewal of tax on privateers' prizes, 99; repeal of above tax, 100-2; request for trade with Americans, 95; welcome of Browne, 126-7, 130

Bascome, George, lawyer of St. Georges: attempt to impede George Bruere, 109, 122; intrigue against Major Anstruther, 127; lawyer in case of *Lord Amherst*, 72; member of anti-privateering association, 85-6; member of assembly's committee on embargo, 43; member of committee of correspondence with agent, 94; of committee on prize tax, 101; of committee for theft of powder, 48; opinion of Bermudian policy, 130; reputation, 43n.

Bermuda, Bermudians: agriculture, 1-2; aid to Americans in war, 54-5, 59-60, 105-7; American plans to seize, 60 and 60n., 129-30; anti-privateering association, 85-6, 87, 95, 101, 128; camp fever, 92; carrying trade, 3-6; commencement of privateering, 123-4, 128-9; description, 1; fisheries, 2; government of, 17-22; lack of respect for government, 13; local patriotism, 13; own view of policy in war, 130-1; religion, 11-12; scarcity of food in 1779-80, 88-92; ship-building and navigation, 3; wrecking, 6

Brimage, William, temporary chief justice, 104

Browne, William, governor of Bermuda: appointment, 116, 125; harmony with assembly, 127, 130; indifference to illicit trade, 128; instructions, 125; reception, 125-6

Bruere, Frances, marriage to Henry Tucker, Jr., 32-3

Bruere, George James, governor of Bermuda 1764-80: attempt to control embargo, 63; character, 23; charges against in 1772, 34n. and 35n.; conduct at theft of powder, 50-1; control of salvage in affair of Spanish vessel, 73;

Index

71; repression by troops and privateers, 82-4, 87-8

Council of Bermuda: composition, 17; conduct about a despatch vessel, 51; conduct in affair of powder, 50; continuing difficulties with George Bruere, 107, 122; dispute with assembly, 1769-72, 30-6; protests against repression of contraband by sloops of war, 76-7; purge by George Bruere, 102-3; question of ports of entry, 25-6; sympathy of five members with Americans, 59

Crow Lane (Hamilton): port of entry, 8, 25, 29; quarter sessions, 24; meeting for election of delegates to Lord Howe, 77; meeting to form association against privateers, 85-6

Crown lands: mismanagement of sale, 19, 34n.; yield, 20

Customs: collection in Bermuda, 6-7; controversy over ports of entry, 7-8, 24-5, 34n., 117; controversy over searchers, Thomas Butterfield, 25n., John Stiles, 26, Joseph Laborn, 121, Paul Bascome, 121, 127

Dartmouth, Earl of, Colonial Secretary, coolness to complaints of Bermuda assembly, 35-6

Davis, Lieutenant David of garrison of Bermuda, 105, 108, 121-2

Dean, Silas, visit to Bermuda and report, 59-60

Deming, the Rev. Oliver, minister of Warwick Presbyterian church, 12

Devonshire, parish: agriculture in, 2; refusal to participate in election of delegates to petition Continental Congress, 42; repudiates appeal to Congress, 44

Dickinson, Thomas of Crow Lane: Justice of the Peace, 24, 35n.; member of assembly and framer of complaints against council and Bruere, 33-6; signature of petition, 42n.

Dispatch, sloop hired by Tuckers, 55-7

Drew, lieutenant of H.M.S. *Scorpion* and affair of rice, 63-4

East Florida, emigration to, 9 and 9n.

Ely's Harbor, port of entry, 8, 34n., 68, 77

Esten, John, judge of court of vice-admiralty: remuneration, 21; resignation, 67; view of advent of George Bruere, 99

Finance in Bermuda: complaints of assembly about in 1772, 34n., 35n.; difficulties of, 20-2; question of receiver-general, 32-6; reorganization by George Bruere, 104

Fisheries, restrictions on, 34n., 35n., 124

Forbes, George, councillor, 19, 39n., 69, 76

Fortifications: controversy between governor and assembly over, 78-9; investigation by legislature, 96; repair and strengthening, 124, 130

Franklin, Benjamin: letter from, 48; negotiation with Colonel Henry Tucker, 47

Gage, General Thomas, report of Bruere to, 51-2

Galatea, sloop of war suppressing contraband in Bermuda, 66-70

Garrison of Bermuda: complaint about, by assembly, 93; need for hospital, 100, 124, 128; reinstatement during American war and employment in aid of customs,

Index

139

THE FOLLOWING LIST OF PERSONS WHO PLAY NO GREAT PART IN THE STORY MAY BE OF SOME GENEALOGICAL INTEREST TO BERMUDIANS

Some of these may refer to two persons of the same name whom I have not been able to distinguish.

Kerr, Wilfred Brenton, 1896–1950.
  Bermuda and the American Revolution, 1760–1783.
₁Hamden, Conn.₁ Archon Books, 1969 ₁ᶜ1936₁

  xii, 142 p. map. 22 cm.

  Includes bibliographical references.

  1. Bermuda Islands—History. 2. U. S.—History—Revolution—
Foreign public opinion. ɪ. Title.

  F1636.K47 1969   972.99   69–19216
  SBN 208–00794–6   MARC

  Library of Congress   ₁7₁